HEARD AMID THE GUNS

True Stories from
the Western Front,
1914–1918

JACQUELINE LARSON
CARMICHAEL

*For Jesse,
Warm Regards*

Heritage House Publishing Company Ltd.
heritagehouse.ca

Cataloguing information available from Library and Archives Canada
978-1-77203-337-3 (pbk)
978-1-77203-338-0 (ebook)

Edited by Renée Layberry
Proofread by Nandini Thaker
Cover and interior book design by Setareh Ashrafologhalai
Cover image: Harold Monks, mid-1917 at Camp Petawawa. Raymond Harlan Brewster, Canadian Letters and Images Project.
Map of France, 1915, on page iii by the Geographical Section, General Staff (GSGS), British War Office. Author's collection.

The interior of this book was produced on FSC®-certified paper, processed chlorine free and acid free.

Heritage House gratefully acknowledges that the land on which we live and work is within the traditional territories of the Lkwungen (Esquimalt and Songhees), Malahat, Pacheedaht, Scia'new, T'Sou-ke, and W̱SÁNEĆ (Pauquachin, Tsartlip, Tsawout, Tseycum) Peoples.

We acknowledge the financial support of the Government of Canada through the Canada Book Fund (CBF) and the Canada Council for the Arts, and the Province of British Columbia through the British Columbia Arts Council and the Book Publishing Tax Credit.

24 23 22 21 20   1 2 3 4 5

Printed in Canada

CONTENTS

▲ *Saskatchewan rancher Charles W.C. Chapman in uniform (left) and George Anderson "Black Jack" Vowel on his wedding day in Hanna, Alberta, 1920 (right).*

PROLOGUE
TWO GRANDFATHERS

IN 2016, a hundred years after the Battle of the Somme, a clerk at the Enterprise Rent-A-Car counter in Amsterdam smiled broadly at me. "You rescued us—twice!" she said. She had just learned that I was Canadian.

"You're welcome," I said, smiling in return.

On a research trip to Belgium and France, I was about to experience the powerful effect the former Western Front in Flanders, Belgium, and France had on my ancestors. The two major arenas of the First World War were within an hour's drive of each other. I was startled by the close proximity of the places my grandfathers fought, where waves of hundreds of thousands of soldiers poured over the gently rolling landscape. That land is still, in many cases, pitted with craters and trenches. Each year, bomb disposal units find thousands of kilograms of unexploded ammunition on the former Western Front. So, when a sign says DO NOT WALK ON THE GRASS, I don't walk on the grass.

Things I had long been told about my grandfather, Oklahoma-born George "Black Jack" Vowel, led me to even more questions. I knew that he died in his early sixties when his tractor overturned on him in the Peace River Valley. I knew the wartime words penned in letters to Louisa "Bebe" Watson Small Peat lived on: CBC Radio based a radio program on them in 1992, and then Peat's daughter gave them to my aunt, Peggy Aston, who passed them along to me. I had transcribed them for a number of articles in the *Edmonton Sun*, *Alberta Views*, and other publications, eventually giving George "Black Jack" Vowel a social media persona and tweeting his words as if I were him, in an effort to tell a new generation about his life in the trenches of the First World War. But being in the trenches where he and my maternal grandfather both fought—that was a different experience altogether.

I am the second-generation product of two soldiers of the First World War. Both grandfathers, prairie ranchers, were in the war for the four-plus years that Canada fought—like so many others. They survived, but they never talked about it. Despite the surface similarities of their backgrounds, the war impacted them in very different ways—ways that would be handed down (for better or worse), like psychological heirlooms, to their children and their children's children.

Somewhere in the trenches of Flanders, on the rolling hills of the Vimy countryside, and in Black Jack's letters and journals, I hoped to find answers to the questions that had been sparked within me.

Charles Wellington Camden Chapman

My maternal grandfather, Charles Wellington Camden Chapman, was a young Saskatchewan rancher at the outset of the Great War, and a volunteer who signed up in November 1914.

The cowboy son of an Anglican minister and adventurer, raised partly in the far north of Churchill, Manitoba, Charlie was an artillery man, operating a gun that lobbed eighteen-pound shells at "Fritz," as the German Imperial Army was dubbed. He was wounded in the leg on October 13, 1915, and shrapnel from the shell was embedded in his back. He was hospitalized for sixty-nine days.

After occupying Germany, Chapman came home whole, as far as you could tell, despite his obvious wound. He had a slight limp in his walk and was a bit hard of hearing. Every so often he'd go to the veterans' hospital, and they'd take another piece of shrapnel out.

He had kind blue eyes that crinkled at the corners and a hearty laugh that rattled in a chest damaged by mustard gas. He married a lovely Canadian girl named Ruth Showalter, who was of French and German stock. Photos with their six kids show a happy family. But Maidstone, Saskatchewan, was a Dust Bowl bust, so they sold the farm for the price of a rickety Ford Model A, into which they loaded up the clan, with suitcases tied to the running boards and mattresses strapped on top, like Joads from Steinbeck's *Grapes of Wrath*.

They went to Ladysmith, Nanaimo, and ultimately Port Alberni, British Columbia, where Grandpa Charlie used a particular trick for getting a job: If you're standing in a job line with hundreds of other men, and if they ask you if you have experience doing X, say "Yes!" even if you don't; figure out how to do X later. Eventually, he finished his career as a foreman at Bloedel, Stewart & Welch's chipper plant. He was a good Royal Canadian Legion man, but he never talked about the war. In fact, he tried to forget about the war. When Charlie Chapman's kids asked him if he killed any Germans in the war, he grinned and said he only practised on bully beef tins.

He was either a loyal hero or a glutton for punishment: Even after four long years in the First World War, he wanted to volunteer for the

Second World War. Told he was too old to enlist, he served in the home militia. He didn't have a perfect life, but he was a genuinely nice guy—cheerful, kind, nurturing, beloved by his children and grandchildren. Charlie Chapman outlived three wives, but not his sense of humour. He bore his decline gracefully and played a mean harmonica with dignity in the kitchen band at the seniors' home in Parksville. He numbered among his friends Tommy Douglas, founder of the NDP and Canada's socialized medicine.

And upon his death, he was laid to a hero's rest with his fellow veterans in Port Alberni's Field of Honour—not far from the resting place of his brother-in-law, First World War veteran Guy Showalter—under the shadow of a tree grown from an acorn that came from Vimy Ridge.

Another grandfather, a very different story.

Louisa "Bebe" Watson Small Peat

Throughout much of the war, my paternal grandfather, George "Black Jack" Vowel, kept up a correspondence with an Irish woman who was destined to become Canada's most high-profile war bride of the Great

War. He wasn't alone in his bid to keep the letters coming in. According to the United Kingdom's Royal Mail, an average of 19,000 mailbags crossed the English Channel every day in 1917. The Royal Mail's Home Depot was handling twelve million letters and a million parcels at its wartime peak, and an estimated two billion letters were addressed to or from servicemen during the war. Even after Armistice, a November 16, 1918 postmark on a postcard from France was still calibrated to urge the public to FEED THE GUNS WITH WAR BONDS.

George's early letters to Miss Bebe, as he called her, showed a sort of rough-hewn charm—some magnetism under the displaced rancher exterior. His language was direct, with a homespun charm. "As we are getting used to the mud, we are feeling better, we all are as happy as a pig fed on tater peelings," he wrote. On a stubborn fellow soldier: "He is just like Paddy's pig. You can coax but he doesn't drive worth a darn." On veering off topic: "If I don't quit drifting I'll get clear off my range."

Bebe asked George to describe himself. His response was self-deprecating: "I look like a loose button on an overcoat."

On the other hand, George wasn't beyond stretching the facts to impress a girl. Embellishments in the letters he wrote to Bebe, according to family records, included the romanticized claims to be a Texas native (he was born in Kansas), fully Irish (his mother's name was French), and an accomplished horse breaker (family members recalled he had little patience with horses, compared to his brother Fred).

A huge picture of Louisa "Bebe" Watson Small Peat on her wedding day hangs in the Canadian War Museum in Ottawa. An Irish-born author and lecturer, lovely and well-spoken, she married Private

Harold R. Peat, a hero who had to up his weight to enlist, campaigned for enlistment, and eventually became the author of *Private Peat*. Bebe wrote the book *Mrs. Private Peat* in 1918, a memoir of her early married life. She devoted two pages to George Vowel, and she saved his letters. "Jack Vowel's letters are in themselves an epitome of the war. He has a power of description, a sense of contrast, and a sense of humour, rarely combined," she wrote.

Bebe's letters to him didn't survive—they were bits of kind encouragement worn to shreds by repeated readings, no doubt. Perhaps they dissolved when French rains waterlogged the entire world (as far as the soldiers were concerned), or jettisoned when he needed to make room for hoarded bits of food.

Holiday Truce

Numerous so-called holiday truces were widely reported in 1914, with men from the two opposing sides briefly emerging from trenches into No Man's Land to exchange cigarettes, sweets, and drink, to show pictures of their sweethearts and families, and even to play a game of football.

"Fraternization" was quickly forbidden by those who wanted the war finished instead of stopped, but the trenches of both sides were so close together they could hear each other for exchanges such as the one George "Black Jack" Vowel described in one of his letters to Louisa "Bebe" Watson Small Peat. One New Year's Eve, he was witness to a fleeting moment of a rare holiday truce. "Say, talk about fireworks!" George wrote. "I was on guard when New Year made her appearance. The grandest display of fireworks ever let loose at once. On the stroke of twelve, 5,000 rifles cracked, flares by hundreds shot into the air. Reckon that was the signal. The artillery opened up. The country was lit for miles. After a couple minutes, it died down quick as it started. Gordie stuck his head over the parapet and wished Fritz a Happy New Year. Fritz's answer was typical: a hail of bullets. I yells across No Man's Land, 'Fritz, you got any resolutions?' Fritz shouts asking if we have any. So I yells back in true spirit of camaraderie, 'It isn't time for us yet, but when weather permits we will make resolutions toward Berlin!' Fritz pulls triggers and makes unprintable remarks about British pigs. As we're not British, we let it pass."

What Happened at the Front

It was the opposite of a bucket list, the list of things that happened to those at the Front. The things George Vowel described were almost unbelievable in their sum total, but they were borne out repeatedly in the memoirs of other soldiers. On one particularly fraught day in 1915, he noted, "Germans sent over 10,000 shells in hour and a half... So damn homesick I can hardly do any work."

When he wasn't delivering rations to the Front or dodging bullets and mortar fire, he wrote. "Bullets ripped the dirt up all round me but none of them were marked Black Jack." Buried by a shell explosion, he clawed his way out of a collapsed dugout, only to fall into a rain-filled shell hole and almost drown, panicking after bumping up against the rubbery flesh of dead soldiers.

He was gassed when the Germans weaponized chlorine. He came down with mumps and the Spanish flu and German measles and trench foot. He wrote about "our trench companions": "The dope they gave us for lice took the skin off. Sure, it drove the lice off alright, but the cure's worse than the reason for it." He walked four miles for a bath, and he carried a wounded buddy a mile and a half to medical help. After a brief leave from the Front to go to Britain, George penned a note on December 4, 1915, on YMCA rest camp letterhead, with words that modern psychologists might call a cry for help: "Coming over on the boat I got so darned homesick that I had a notion to jump overboard, but I am alright now... I guess we will be in the ditches on Christmas Day; some prospect to look forward to, eh?"

He earned the British Military Medal for bravery, by one report for single-handedly taking out a bunch of Germans at the Somme, and by another for being handy with the Lewis gun and holding his post at the obliterated Mouquet Farm (which would be rebuilt on the other side of the road after the war). Before-and-after British government aerial photos show devastation on the land at Pozières, where the Allies fought to break the Germans' Thiepval line mid-1916. The original farm was demolished, pulverized beyond recognition. Road gone, trenches gone, farm gone—soldiers gone. George "kept his Lewis Gun working perfectly and was largely responsible for... continued possession of this post," his medal commendation read. There was a world of damage between those lines. The medal lasted; the accompanying promotion did not. War-weary, he took off without permission. He "got the skids put under [him], caught without a permission belt around Abeele." He got into fisticuffs with another soldier and was demoted from the promotion and the Lewis gun trainer position he won when he earned the British Military Medal. "Please address letters to just Private again," he pleaded glumly of his pen pal. Accepting his punishment, he wrote this

cranky haiku: "Drills by Sam Hughes himself. Something seemed to be eating him. Probably lousy [with lice]!"

Something was eating George Vowel: war was wearing him down.

"I am hunkering, trying to make myself small whilst all around me the shells they are a-flyin'... They're strafing again, so if my spelling's bad don't blame me, blame Fritz. I'm doubled up in the corner of the dugout under a hunk of tin, trying to be itty-bitty as possible. The beggars don't care where they throw the darned shells; they are liable to hurt someone yet... Why, just the other day they broke up a perfectly good poker game; shell went off in our midst and injured three of us. I am supposed to be an artist at swearing, but I choke up whenever I start in on the devils... Last week we marched 42 km in a day (a record, by the way, for the Canadian Corps), rain every step. I am sitting on sugar boxes to keep out of the water, with a coke brazier under my feet... if I turn every so often, I reckon I'll get dry eventually."

He was a long way from Hays, Kansas, where he was born. He savoured the memories, wishing to be still a kid there, sipping lemonade from a jelly glass or walking beside the horses plodding in their traces with their soft clop-clops. He recalled shelling purple-hulled peas on the porch in the afternoon in O-o-o-klahoma, where everything was OK and the rumble in the distance was surely thunder, not enemy shelling, in summer's silver-lined electric heat.

Recollections of Christmas past seemed to comfort him somewhat in the trenches. "Xmas Day dawned foggy, wet, and muddy just like many another of the winter days in Flanders. With the occasional bark of a gun breaking in on our festivities to remind us that everything was not as it should be, we had a pretty lively day of it. Last year I spent Christmas on the plains (Alberta). Two years ago I was working in a coal mine in [Crowsnest] Pass, BC. Three years ago, I was working on a ranch in Alberta. Four years ago, two boys and myself rode sixty miles to dance. We got snowed in and stayed a week." And there George was, slogging it out inch for inch at the point of the bayonet, wishing he was anywhere but there.

In 1916, he went to a one-year reunion of the Calgary Highlanders' first trip to the trenches. He left early... and blue. Just a handful— a fraction—of his original comrades remained. "Most of the boys I came with are gone," he wrote. "Not many of the original 10th Battalion left. Lost more of the boys in Festubert on 21 May. I came through alright but words cannot describe the scenes we went through at Ypres. I often

wonder how any of us made it through. We fought six days, four days without food. Some of the boys got no sleep for almost a week... We will win the war in time but at what personal cost?... Sandy Clarke was killed today, he was right beside me; a sniper shot him in the head..."

He didn't spare frank talk of the danger, but he did go easy on the cussing for Bebe's delicate sensibilities. "Fritzy's fighting like a bloody double-distilled son-of-a-seacook... The paper reports 'quiet on the Western Front except for artillery duels.' They didn't consult with us or we might have had something to say on the subject, being we are always the target for these so-called duels."

It would be many decades before the term "post-traumatic stress disorder" would be coined. The words they used on the Front implied a limitation of duration: shell shock, battle fatigue, "going bugs" from terror raining down and nowhere to go but a dugout to try to escape it. "Bugs" was a term George Vowel used in a letter to Bebe.

"The worst? The strain of waiting for something to happen, the slithering whistle of a shell going higher then coming down. A person doesn't really know how they will feel until the time comes. The worst strain is waiting for something to happen, and it's not an uncommon occurrence for men to go crazy under shell fire," he wrote.

"The noise made by high explosives makes your hair stand on end. Along comes flying steel and fragments... The Front is just the place for the person that likes thrills. Let me tell you about shell shock. It starts with cold chills and sinking stomach. Your brain urges your feet to beat it, but your feet won't move and your knees get to wobbling. Then your nerve breaks, and that's when you go bugs. I've seen it and it isn't nice."

Not a particularly religious person back in Canada before or after the war, he was no foxhole atheist, and he attended Protestant services during wartime "church parades." In August of 1915, he described an outdoor service: "The 10th Battalion has a brass band and we had it out to Church Parade today. We hold church in a big wood and it sure sounded out of place."

By this time, he was all too accustomed to the twice-daily dosage of rum, administered by officers, officially sanctioned as the only way to provide a little relief: a sixteenth of a pint per man per day, to be dispensed daily at the Front, at stand-to. It was a measure of oblivion in the midst of sometimes unspeakable horror. If rum was an acquired taste, George acquired it, and would unleash that taste on his future family in years to come. "I wish I could ask Dobbs where the rum is," he wrote to Bebe. "He was toting the section's ration of SRD [Service Rum Diluted] when he was hit, and that's the last we saw of it," he wrote. "Don't go to hell. It's sure to be overrun with rats, lice, and a Tommy [a British soldier] at every fire to keep Fritzy sizzling."

Back home, George was in trouble with his folks. Somebody who had come home from the Front, invalided home perhaps, spread a rumour that they had seen George hunkered over a dead German, carving a cross into the man's chest with his Bowie knife. "Tickled my brother but not Mother," he told Bebe, knowing Ellen Vowel would weep, letting out her hairpins, brushing her long, thin hair at night before bed, in tears at the idea of a damaged boy, feral from war, gouging the bodies of the slain.

Canadian soldiers encountering prospective prisoners of war were known to be particularly brutal. But there was enough recruitment propaganda about Fritz committing atrocities without some joker adding fuel to the fire and spreading tales back home, George knew.

Hot under the collar, George denied the vigilantism—and promised his own revenge, but on the rumour monger. "I'll live to drag a dead cat across somebody's grave yet. Somebody will hear from me," he blustered.

Maybe just to scare the guy, he might bring his Bowie knife.

If George was among those who refused mercy to surrendering Germans, he never wrote about it, nor talked to family about it. In retrospect, it wasn't impossible, this idea that George "Black Jack" Vowel had joined those "revenging" the unsubstantiated legend of the so-called "crucified Canadian soldier"—a Canadian alleged to have been found nailed to a makeshift cross with German bayonets.

Eventually, "Canada's Golgotha" was determined to be a hoax, although in his book, *Private Peat*, Private Harold R. Peat claimed to know somebody (unnamed) who saw it.

Unable to march because of a flaming case of trench foot, George couldn't run supplies at the Front or dodge shells as he had in the first years of the war. With his gunnery skills as a Lewis gun trainer, he was marked to work as a tail gunner in the air. There was a narrow miss when he reported for training as ordered—twice, but his assigned

trainer failed to show up both times. George said he was mad about it, but secretly he may have been relieved. He enjoyed the thrill of the show, and flyboys had aerial thrills, alright—but a terribly low life expectancy. "I have watched them fall right out of the sky and break apart," Vowel wrote.

That was when his cobbler skills came in handy; he first learned to cobble shoes on the family ranch in Oklahoma, where making do by resoling and repairing boots with scraps of harness leather and a few snips and stitches meant adding years of wear. He hammered out a niche for himself as a shoemaker on a little mobile crew of technicians, along with a saddler, an armourer, and a farrier. He hobbled about and was drafted to cook for the group. The war needed bodies, and bodies had feet that needed boots—and it was boots that helped prolong George Vowel's life for a year while his own feet healed.

He remembered his father, proud and stern, on the train platform—no sentimental nonsense about Calloway Vowel; his mother wept quietly, but he could hear her so loud and clear over the urgent clang at

the train station. There was a high, piercing tone ever-present now, the wee gift of shell explosions never completely fading, like a maniac devil fiddling in between the ears, like a shell-scarred church steeple enwreathed with chimes of armistice. His helmet was the bell and his head was the clapper: inside of him a scared kid, inside of him the cry of a wolf, a ringing and a roaring that would never quite hush.

Meanwhile, as the war built to a miserable climax, his letters and journal entries lost any trace of his earlier charming optimism. "The country is blazing with fire. Both sides are seeing just how much ammo they can waste. Fritzy won't find Tommy asleep; the boys are throwing everything but the wheels at him," he wrote.

On Armistice Day, the Hanna, Alberta, rancher underlined the date in his journal: November 11, 1918. He made a single entry in his journal: "returned boots."

After finally occupying Germany (and really enjoying Cologne), George "Black Jack" Vowel made the reverse journey of the one he took almost five years earlier. He crossed the Atlantic in a ship, docked at Halifax, then boarded a train west. He was discharged May 5, 1919, in Toronto. He snapped his war journal shut after writing a curt note: "Arrived home today, finished with the army after four years and nine months' absence."

Marrying Well

Back home in Alberta, the wounded George Vowel lived up to expectations as best as he could. He rejoined his father and brothers in their horse ranching operation. He married a pretty Norwegian immigrant who had been in love with another soldier, a fellow who didn't return to her after the war. Early pictures of George and Laura Knutson Vowel on their honeymoon in Idaho show a couple with love in bloom, picnicking on the grass, a camera nearby for memorable snapshots. Clearly, at this point, she never imagined him, decades later, shooting her dog. She was wooed by his intensity, his deep-set blue eyes, haunted and somehow vulnerable and vivid. He looked at her with such attention, she thought she knew what it meant. She assumed love and patience and understanding and closeness; what a good father he would be to their offspring. His thick dark hair was luxuriant under her fingers; she admired his muscled frame, his farming background, and his dashing profile in uniform. They had so much in common, she thought—both of them came to the Bullpound Country via America as youths, he from Oklahoma, she from Norway via North Dakota. She was quiet, he was quiet—but she didn't know *why* he was quiet. She didn't know about the battery of images flickering behind his eyelids, or that war was both the making and undoing of him. As she put her hair up for their wedding, she dreamed of building a farm and a family with her handsome veteran husband. Their wedding notice in the paper was all "Mr. and Mrs. Happy Honeymooning in Idaho."

The children came soon enough. This seemed to be where things started to fall apart. The first was a boy, blond curls tousled, bright blue eyes merry. But fatherhood was another kind of trench. George teased the child mercilessly, excluding him for the slightest offence, engaging him in battle. Laura was wary but hapless, and she begged for fatherly compassion, for truce. She was as compassionate as she could be, walking on eggshells amid his ragings, blaming herself. She could hardly blame the war, as he would never talk about it.

More children quickly followed, the Depression on their heels. There was limited paid work, limited food, limited money—but unlimited bitterness. George's taste for booze, nurtured for years in the trenches, made him itchy with a misery that was unscratchable. His wrath was a pit, a dugout, a shell hole with iron stakes at the bottom, things he couldn't bear to talk about. And when his buddies came for a visit—old friends, or the few left after the chaos of war, the few who knew what the chaos was, from the good old bad old days in the trenches—they would sit at the lake. Catch fish or not. Get "good and drunk." But he couldn't be both good and drunk. George was a mean drunk. Funny first, then mean. Growing boys weren't allowed. Growing boys were punished harshly for asking, and treated like hired help. In peacetime, the chaos was still there, just different: it meant five growing kids who needed their holey shoes lined with carboard to keep out the dirt and cold. The battle now was eking out a living in a Dust Bowl drought, the skirmishes fought with the price per ton of grain. It was hard, perhaps, to sympathize with his kids who, despite

the deprivations of the Great Depression, still had it easier than the poor devils who never made it home after giving it their full measure.

Laura wondered: Why should their oldest son cringe in the corner, hiding tears behind his blond curls, as if his father's stern manner meant he didn't love him? Why did George bellow? Why was he a mean drunk instead of a jovial one? He seemed to take the attitude that life was hard, the rations few. Were the guns in the distant past almost as loud to him with peace at every turn as they ever were on the Western Front? Was the buzz in his own head keener still to him now, more than any other sound? Was he ever a boy, or was he his father's created ranch hand, as his son was to him? Did his father apply the iron of his will to break his? When as a boy he grew to be muscled, was he ready for a harness as far as his own father was concerned? Was he told to quit school to help on the farm? Did war start this? How many generations of a family can the parasite of war work its way through?

From high hopes to last hopes to no hopes, Laura put up with the tumult. Endured the chaos. Tried to get the kids to be good, to be quiet. But when the last of them were safely out of school, she left him.

Because he shot her dog. Because they say what a bully does to a wall or an animal, he'd like to do to someone else. And because sometimes love is not enough and there was no language for what dogged George. No therapy. No diagnosis. No treatment. And when he died a decade later, she shed her tears at a distance. Tears for him, for her. For their children, scarred by their father's searing disinterest. For the oldest son, who went on to drink heavily and roar at his own children. Tears for all the men, for all the sons and daughters cut down for generations. For an eternal onslaught of emotions over a phantom war that was never quite over.

Genealogist and researcher Annette Fulford has interviewed hundreds of descendants of war brides for her blog and a book on the same subject. Undiagnosed post-traumatic stress disorder played a role in the disintegration of some of the unions of the returning soldiers, she said: "There were some returning soldiers who couldn't deal with life—and a few brides who had to get rescued by their parents."

For others, there was no rescue.

On CNN in April 2017, Christal Presley, author of *Thirty Days with My Father: Finding Peace from Wartime PTSD*, said even in the modern day, the impact of PTSD on the next generation is underestimated. "There has been such a focus on veterans and PTSD in the media, which is great, but somehow the missing piece is how that PTSD also affects a person's family," Presley said.

A generation later, George's eldest son John didn't go off to the Second World War, much to John's bitter disappointment; he was ruled 4F—unfit for military service—due to his poor vision and childhood rickets. George's second son, Don, would be an underage volunteer for

the Second World War. An older soldier Don met in the war in Europe told him about his dad, old "Black Jack," in the Great War. "There was never a better soldier ever lived," the army buddy told him. "Black Jack wasn't afraid of anything—he had more guts than a slaughterhouse." (Black Jack's letters, some scrawled in terror while hunkered under a piece of tin and "trying to make [him]self as small as possible" in the slaughterhouses of the Somme, Festubert, Cambrai, St. Eloi, Mount Sorrel, Passchendaele, Kitcheners' Wood, Saint-Julien, Thiepval, Albert, and Arras suggest differently.)

I descend from two First World War veterans. Two grandfathers. One from each side of the family. So much in common—prairie ranchers who never met. For one, the First World War was the making of him. For the other, the war was the making of him and then the breaking of him—and almost the end of him. I wonder about the differences in their lives. What is between the threads of their wartime experiences that I don't know about?

Yesteryear's Social Media

Some 59,544 of the soldiers serving with the Canadian Expeditionary Force died in the war. Almost three times that many went home physically wounded. Time would reveal that for many, the psychological scars were far more difficult to heal. Returning wounded in heart, the boys they once used to be wanted their years back. Subsequent generations might want the same thing.

In these young soldiers' postcards, journals, and letters, we have permanent records of the social media of yesteryear; it was just slower, analog all the way. This was how they tweeted: a postcard trundled across continents and oceans, into a cast-iron mailbox. Pen, paper. A note scratched out by a fellow sprawled on sodden trench floors, ignoring his peers as he texts home. All that was missing was a keyboard. Cancelled stamps hanging on for dear life through onioned layers of handling. Instead of a drop-down menu of "who should see this,"

letters were posted, censored, carried by cart and in the bellies of ships, delivered, ripped open, pressed in scrapbooks, shown over tea, cradled in fingertips at the market. No Facebook posts or texts—journal entries. Their memes? Propaganda posters to influence and persuade. Bad news? Not a voicemail but a telegram, crumpled in distress, abandoned damp on a hall table. Or the dreaded sorry-to-inform-you knock on the door. If he was gone, there was a photo on the mantel instead of a selfie on Instagram. And no GoFundMe for the widow and her children.

Walking on the Western Front, descending into preserved trenches, visiting museums, sifting through the social media of 1914–1919, and talking with the descendants of other veterans, I heard so many fascinating stories from so many different perspectives. I wanted to present as many as possible, if only because the questions linger: We may know what they did in the war, but what did war do in them?

TIMELINE

JUNE 28

While parading through crowds in Sarajevo, Austrian Archduke Franz Ferdinand and his wife Sophie are assassinated by Serbian nationalists. Nations begin lining up behind the world's top economic powers. The Triple Entente powers: France, Russia, the United Kingdom of Great Britain and Ireland. The Central Powers: Germany and Austria-Hungary.

1914

▲ *A plea to Canadian women to send the men of the household to in turn keep the German Imperial Army from the door.* ARCHIVES OF ONTARIO, I0016138

▲ *Soldiers depart for training camp at Valcartier, QC.* C.L. MULLEN COLLECTION, CANADIANLETTERS.CA

➤ *Enthusiastic recruits enlisting at the Toronto recruiting centre as Canada goes to war in August 1914.* TORONTO STAR FILE

JULY 28

Austria declares war on Serbia. Russia sides with Serbia.

AUGUST 1

Germany declares war on Russia and France, invading neutral Belgium on the way to invade France.

AUGUST 4

Great Britain declares war on Germany; her colony, Newfoundland and Labrador, are in it as well. Between the Royal Newfoundland Regiment, the Newfoundland Royal Naval Reserve, and the Newfoundland Forestry Corps, as well as the Canadian Expeditionary Force, almost 12,000 enlisted, plus another 500 in the merchant marine, as well as 500 nurses. More than one in ten of those who served perished.

Canada declares she's automatically at war, too. From a nation of just eight million souls spread widely, more than 600,000 will don uniforms; one in ten won't come home, and almost one in three will be injured.

For all, the psychological scars will remain uncounted and uncountable.

AUGUST 22

Canada's *War Measures Act* is passed. A statute of the Parliament of Canada, it provides for declaration of war, invasion, insurrection, and emergency measures. Controversy swirls over the suspension of civil liberties and personal freedoms, especially with the internment of people suspected of hostile allegiances because of their ethnic or national origins.

OCTOBER 1

The First Canadian Division sails for Britain. From October to November 1914, the First Battle of Ypres rages in Belgium. Germany fails to reach the English Channel, foreshadowing four more years of the same.

NOVEMBER 1

Four Canadians killed with the sinking of HMS *Goodhope* in the Battle of Coronel off Chile are the first Canadians killed in action.

From 1914 to 1917, two opposing armies will be basically deadlocked on the 600-mile Western Front in the trenches of Belgium and France.

APRIL 22–MAY 25

One telltale sign that the war is dragging on the Western Front: successive numbers issued to repeated battles over the same patch of ground. The Second Battle of Ypres sees 6,000 Canadian casualties and the grim introduction of chemical warfare as German troops pipe in chlorine at Kitcheners' Wood.

Local civilian populations are evacuated, fighting erupted at Gravenstafel, Saint-Julien, Frezenberg, and Bellewaerde Ridge.

FEBRUARY 16

The spring of 1915 is a bloody one all around. After landing in France, the First Canadian Division is soon engaged in the fight for the Western Front in France and Belgium. The battles come in quick succession, bang-bang-bang.

1915

MARCH 10

The Battle of Neuve Chapelle.

MARCH 14–15

A fight at St. Eloi.

APRIL 26

Italy leaves the Triple Alliance.

MAY

The Second Battle of Artois sees soldiers sending letters home from places like Aubers, Festubert, and Givenchy in France.

MAY 7

A German U-boat sinks the luxury ocean passenger liner *Lusitania* in a move that will gain the Triple Entente global sympathy and lead, eventually, to the US entering the war two years later.

MAY 23

Italy declares war on Austria-Hungary.

SEPTEMBER–OCTOBER 1915

The Third Battle of Artois sees fighting centred at Loos, Bois-Grenier, the Hohenzollern Redoubt.

▲ *Canadian troops at the demolished town of Lievin, France, five miles from Vimy Ridge.* THOMAS FRANKLIN TOWNSEND COLLECTION, CANADIANLETTERS.CA

SEPTEMBER 17

The Second Canadian Division arrives in France.

The landscape's shell holes are rearranged to resemble a desolate lunar landscape as fresh artillery barrages from both sides. The number of crosses at graves continues to mount. Reinforcements pour in, fresh fodder for the guns.

While death and destruction drones on across the Western Front, soldiers are deployed to other global hotspots as well: Macedonia from 1915 to 1917, the Dardanelles, Egypt, and Palestine from 1915 to 1916.

▲ *Loading the guns for the 5th Battery of the Canadian Garrison Artillery on the Albert–Bapaume Road near Pozieres in 1916.* THOMAS FRANKLIN TOWNSEND COLLECTION, CANADIANLETTERS.CA

FEBRUARY 21–DECEMBER 18

The Battle of Verdun is the largest, most costly one between the Germans and the French. Casualty estimates (both wounded and killed, on both sides) for the protracted fight approach a million. A memorial ossuary houses the remains of 130,000 soldiers of both the French and the German sides whose remains were indistinguishable.

1916

MARCH–APRIL

The deadly battle at St. Eloi Craters.

JUNE 2–JUNE 13

The Battle of Mount Sorrel leaves about 8,000 Canadian casualties.

▲ *Soldiers make collectible trench art from widely available materials—shells.*
THE MULLEN COLLECTION

JULY 1

Canada's Dominion Day. The bloody Battle of the Somme opens.

Of 780 sent into Beaumont-Hamel from the Newfoundland Regiment, 684 are killed or wounded.

The Battle of the Somme lasts until November 18; the Canadians come into the fray in September. Almost a million lads are dead by the battle's end. There are 24,029 Canadian casualties. Somme battles include: Albert, Bazentin Ridge, Fromelles, High Wood, Pozières, Guillemont, Ginchy, Flers-Courcelette, Thiepval Ridge, Le Transloy, Ancre Heights (the capture of Regina Trench).

▲ *Recovering Canadians practice therapeutic knitting while recovering from battle wounds in France.* THOMAS FRANKLIN TOWNSEND COLLECTION/CANADIANLETTERS.CA

It's a global thing: Despite neutral pockets and countries, every continent and all oceans are in the war.

1917

FEBRUARY

Germany goes all-in in submarine warfare to control the North Atlantic—the final nail in the coffin for American neutrality.

FEBRUARY–MARCH 2017

In Russia, growing antipathy toward the Romanov dynasty, compounded by Great War miseries, leads to the February Revolution.

MARCH 15

With the Revolution afoot, Russian tsar Nicholas II abdicates. His family is taken prisoner, to later be executed by the Bolsheviks in 1918.

APRIL–JUNE

The Battle of Arras blazes. Vimy Ridge, First Scarpe, Second Scarpe, La Coulotte, Arleux, Third Scarpe, the Affairs South of the Souchez River, and Avion.

● APRIL 6

America abandons the bid to keep
out of the war. Spurred on by
pro-war sentiment and fuelled by the
Zimmermann Telegram, the sinking
of civilian liners, and the German navy
stepping up their game for all-out
war in the Atlantic, disrupting traffic
and commerce, the US Congress
overcomes latent anti-British sentiment among some sectors and votes
to declare war on Germany, and
Germany only. Over the remainder of
the war, they will pour more than four
million soldiers into the war effort, a
winning infusion.

● JUNE–DECEMBER

The Third Battle of Ypres goes over
the same region yet again, with
the hotbeds of Messines, Pilckem
Ridge, Langemark, Menin Road
Ridge, Polygon Wood, Broodseinde,
Poelcappelle, First and Second
Passchendaele, and Cambrai.

● APRIL 9–APRIL 12

Starting on Easter Sunday, the Triple
Entente powers surprise the Germans
by setting the countryside ablaze
in the Battle of Vimy Ridge. The
Canadians use "creeping barrage" to
storm and seize the ridge, with British
and French help. There are 10,602
Canadian casualties.

● AUGUST 15–25

The Battle of Hill 70 is on.

● AUGUST 29

Conscription passes in Canada.

YOURS
not to do and die -
Yours but to go and
BUY
VICTORY
BONDS
1918

▲ *A Canadian poster urges those on the home front to give money since they don't have to go in harm's way.* ARCHIVES OF ONTARIO, 10016144

● OCTOBER 26–NOVEMBER 14
The Canadian Corps is engaged at the Battle of Passchendaele.

● DECEMBER 6
Devastation and loss are off the charts as the Halifax Explosion kills 1,631 when a munitions ship collides with another vessel in harbour. Haligonians rush to watch the fireworks, causing a second wave of tragedy upon subsequent explosions. This sends Canada's civilian war dead numbers skyrocketing; the numbers dead in Halifax alone will ultimately swell to 1,782.

● DECEMBER 7
The Americans declare war on German ally Austria-Hungary.

● DECEMBER 17
The Canadian federal election is polarized by conscription in a nation of voters reeling from wartime losses.

● JANUARY 1918–DECEMBER 1920

The deadly so-called Spanish flu pandemic is aided in part by the movement of ships and trains full of crowded troops. It's not a Spanish virus, specifically, but government string-pulling generates fake news; Spain, whose neutrality in the war irritates higher-ups to no end, is the only place the media is permitted to report on what is actually a worldwide pandemic—which makes the whole thing look like Spain's fault. An incredible half-billion people worldwide are infected with the unusually deadly virus—including those in the Arctic and on Pacific Islands in the middle of nowhere. Death estimates range from 20 to 50 million.

In 1918, other First World War theatres open up: North-West Persia, the Caspian, Murmansk, Archangel, and Siberia.

1918

A Canada Post stamp honouring William George Barker from Dauphin, MB. The Victoria Cross ace's severe wounds from a crash restricted the use of his legs and an arm; he died young in a plane crash. A plaque on his tomb reads, "The most decorated war hero in the history of Canada, the British Empire, and the Commonwealth of Nations."
© CANADA POST CORPORATION 2019.
REPRODUCED WITH PERMISSION.

● MARCH–JUNE

The German Offensives consume the Western Front, shifting to France— the Somme, places like St. Quentin, Crossings, First Bapaume, Rosières.

The First Battle of Arras sees fierce losses at Hamel, the Lys, Estaires, Hazebrouck, and Messines, as well as the Loss of Hill 63 and the First Kemmel Ridge, and the action of La Becque.

● AUGUST

The beginning of the end—the turning point—is the Battle of Amiens, spearheaded by the Canadian Corps, with 9,074 Canadian casualties.

The Hundred Days Offensive. The Allies' Advance to Victory puts the Germans in retreat. They fight over familiar ground, with the Second Battles of the Somme, Albert, and the Second Bapaume, Second Battles of Arras and Scarpe at Monchy-le-Preux. There are bitter contests at Drocourt-Quéant Canal, the Battles of the Hindenburg Line, Havrincourt, Épehy, Canal du Nord (capture of Bourlon Wood), St. Quentin Canal, Beaurevoir Line, Cambrai, Pursuit to the Selle, Courtrai, the Selle, Valenciennes with the capture of Moot Hill, the Sambre, Passage of the Grande Honnelle, the Capture of Mons. The Triple Entente forces are ordered to keep up the attack to the bitter end.

● NOVEMBER 11

Finally, Armistice stops the shooting and shelling at 11 AM and scarcely a moment sooner. Over nine million service personnel and twenty million civilians have been killed in war. More would die unnaturally soon from wounds and the grim after-effects. Despite the ceasefire, complete extrication of prisoners of war on both sides takes a lot longer. At great effort and cost, America repatriates almost 50,000 of her dead, soldiers who were already twice buried where they fell. The remainder of over 110,000 dead are either buried in Europe, or their names are inscribed where the missing are recognized. By national decree, Canada's dead—more than 61,000—remain where they fell.

1919

JUNE 28

After six months of Allied negotiations at the Paris Peace Conference and occupying Germany, Canada signs the Treaty of Versailles—five years to the day after Archduke Franz Ferdinand's assassination. Article 231, the crippling "War Guilt Clause," requires Germany to disarm and to make USD 33 billion in reparations, the equivalent of over USD 495 billion today. The arrangements please hardly anybody at the table, judged too hard or too soft on the Germans, depending on which side you are on. Among the German population, a conspiracy theory arises. Egged on by nationalist sentiment, anti-Semitism, and the pain of reparations, the "stabbed in the back" myth suggests the German army had still been in the war and was even about to win when it was betrayed. As the myth grows, the ground is laid for the rise of the Third Reich and Nazi rule under a disgruntled German soldier of the Great War: Adolf Hitler.

Exchange and repatriation of prisoners of war continues for many

➤ *The League of Nations Armenia Commission, June 19, 1925. From left are G. Carle, Fridtjof Nansen, and C.E. Dupuis (seated), and Vidkun Quisling and Pio Le Savio (standing). The League would never live up to its promise, and in two decades the world would be at war again. Quisling would play Norway into Hitler's hands in the Second World War.* PUBLIC DOMAIN

1920

months after Armistice. In the coming years, veterans who had suffered much would continue to need treatment and deserve (but won't necessarily get) therapy. Too many linger only to die unnaturally early deaths.

In some theatres, including Iraq and Palestine, bodies of the war dead remain unburied for a decade or more because of the slow pace of reconstruction.

JANUARY 1

The League of Nations is founded to fulfill the Treaty of Versailles, its goal is to prevent war through united security and disarmament, and negotiation and arbitration of international differences. The group intends to tackle everything from fair treatment of Indigenous inhabitants, trafficking, the arms trade, POWs, and the protection of minorities. The First World War's Allied countries are permanent executive members. Ultimately ineffective at reaching its goals, the League of Nations is the forerunner of the eventual, more substantial United Nations.

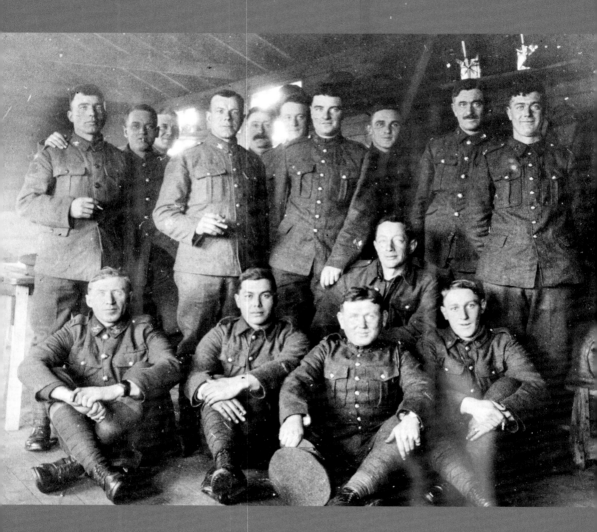

Yukon soldiers, 1917, somewhere on the Western Front.
YUKON ARCHIVES, MAGGIE'S MUSEUM COLLECTION, 82/331 #5

1

GOING ON TO WAR

A Territory Goes to War

At the outbreak of the war, Yukon was a microcosm of Canada. A fledgling territory with the population of a small town, there were about 5,000 men, women, and children over the whole region. It was a rough-and-ready frontier after the Gold Rush. An astonishing 1,100 or so volunteered to serve. They were "a drop in the ocean of the Canadians who served in the expeditionary force during the war—although it was said that Yukon gave its men and its money, its heart and its soul, to the Imperial cause in greater proportion than anywhere else in the country," writes historian Michael Gates in his article in the *Northern Review*, a special collection of papers that were originally presented at a May 2016 conference about "The North and the First World War," held in Whitehorse, Yukon.

In those early days of the twentieth century—before the war and battles like Vimy Ridge knitted the Canadians into a fighting unit with their own identity—many volunteers of British descent still thought of themselves as British citizens, Gates says.

"When war was declared, Commissioner George Black called for volunteers. They opened a ledger book in the lobby... there were sixty-nine names on the list. Only three identified themselves as Canadian, all the other Canadians identified themselves as British," says Gates, the author of six books—including *From the Klondike to Berlin.*

Many Americans slipped across the border to sign up with the Canadian Expeditionary Force in the two-plus years before America entered the war. Many newcomers of other nationalities were also keen to sign up. The Klondike's promise of mineral riches and frontier opportunities drew people from around the world, and there were Americans and other nationalities among the Yukon volunteers. People like Saletto Michunovich of Montenegro, who would return from the Frontier to Europe to take up arms only to perish when the armoured car he was a gunner on was hit by a shell.

It took extra determination for some fellows to enlist. Rowland Bourke of Yukon was rejected by all three branches of the Canadian armed forces because of his eyesight. He returned to his native England, joined the Royal Navy Volunteer Reserve, and received the Victoria Cross for commanding a motor launch to rescue men at sea under heavy fire. Unfortunately, his vessel was hit fifty-five times; he would succumb to his injuries, but many more lives were saved because of his daring.

Another striking Yukon character was Grizzly Bear James Murdoch Christie. At age forty-seven, he lied outright about his age to get into the fray with the Princess Patricia's Light Infantry. Anyone who doubted his fitness for the battlefield would have only to look at his face, reconstructed after his brush with the source of his nickname— that king of predators, a grizzly bear.

"Because of his wilderness skills, he was well-suited in leading teams into No Man's Land, scouting, and sniping," writes Gates. Christie was awarded the Military Cross for covering the attack on an almost impregnable pill box.

Some heroes were as colourful and rough-cut as the young territory itself. Gates chronicles Yukon's most famous Great War volunteer: poet Robert Service. Ruled as 4F on account of varicose veins and advanced age, Service found work first as a war correspondent, then as a volunteer ambulance driver at the Front.

"Eager to get as close to the action as possible, he was once arrested on suspicion of being a spy and almost shot," Gates says in the *Northern Review*. To no one's surprise, the already famous poet had a smash hit on his hands with *Rhymes of a Red Cross Man*, published 1916.

And then there was Joe Boyle. Good at talking people into things, the enterprising Klondike mining millionaire could pull strings. With spoils of wealth secured by outmanoeuvering wealthy American financiers, Boyle financed and recruited the Boyle Machine Gun Detachment—and talked militia minister Sam Hughes into signing off on it. His Yukon lads took honours at Courcelette, the Somme, Vimy Ridge, and Passchendaele. In his spare time, he ran a spy network, forged a peace treaty between Romania and Russia, kickstarted the fractured Russian rail system, and facilitated the return of Romania's national treasury from Russia. In a daring rescue, Boyle took seventy Romanian dignitaries, who were held captive in Ukraine, to freedom in Romania via the Black Sea. In his spare time, he romanced the queen of Romania. Once a humble bouncer in the Monte Carlo saloon in Dawson City, he would eventually receive the Distinguished Service Order from Britain, the French Croix de Guerre, the Russian Order of St. Vladimir, and the Order of the Star of Romania.

Too Young

Private Frederick Freeman Laing of Halifax was not long out of short pants, too young at fourteen, too stubborn for his own good. Determined to go to the Great War battlefields, he sneaked aboard the SS *Caledonian*, along with stowaways Dr. Leo Landry, Dr. Augustine McNulty, Dr. Joseph Molloy, E. Carroll, Thomas O'Meara, and A. Shaw. He was felled as a sapling, dismantling his folks' dreams, and would forever remain a Halifax schoolboy. He was first interred where he fell on May 11, 1916, a still-green leaf among the maples. His grave was violently destroyed a month later, along with 229 others. Frederick Laing's second stone at Maple Copse Cemetery says, KNOWN TO BE BURIED HERE and THEIR GLORY SHALL NOT BE BLOTTED OUT. Freddie, we hardly knew ye.

Shells tore up the graveyard during the Battle of Mount Sorrel. Troops then had to go in "working parties" to re-inter the bodies, prompting the inscription KNOWN TO BE BURIED HERE. Will Bird's memoir *And We Go On* describes this grim work in piercing detail.

Charles Henry Savage of Eastman, Quebec, had enlisted with the 5th Canadian Rifles in 1915. He describes in his memoir, *And So We Joined the Army*, the working party debacle of re-interring the bodies of young Nova Scotia runaway Frederick Freeman Laing and others ripped from their graves by repeated shelling at Maple Copse in the month since Laing's first burial: "All work of this sort had to be done at night and under severe machine gun and shell fire, but even had this not been the case, Maple Copse still would have presented an almost impossible task. What had once been a thick wood was now a tumbled mass of blasted trees and upturned earth, and among this debris were the bodies of hundreds of Canadians and Germans. The ground had been fought over almost continuously for twelve days during hot and rainy weather, and the stench from it was sickening. A poor place to give men their first taste of war. Certainly it was no psychologist who ordered these working parties."

Three Years a Prisoner in Germany

Major J.C. Thorn was among the first Canadians to sign up to fight. On April 24, 1915, surrounded by dead and wounded fellow soldiers, he was taken prisoner by the Germans near Saint-Julien. "Swarms of Germans were coming at me with their bayonets," he wrote. He was able to tear up maps of trenches and redoubts he had in pockets before a search began. His book, *Three Years a Prisoner in Germany*, outlines his multiple attempts to escape prison camp in Mecklenburg, Germany. Tunnelling out, being wheeled out in baskets or in a wheelbarrow, even dressing as a widow, all failed. He got the farthest in the widow disguise, complete with a boned corset and a wig, all fashioned with the help of his fellow prisoners. After multiple escapes, recaptures, and transports to different facilities, he was eventually released through a prisoner exchange in 1918. He was sent home to Canada on the word of doctors who found him to be a "nervous wreck" with deafness caused by weaponized chlorine gas days before he was taken into captivity.

2

WARTIME RACISM

I N THE CURRENT day, it's shocking to think of soldiers being sorted by ethnicity, but in the First World War, discrimination was a legal part of the system. The powers that be were frequently hung up on ethnic origins. Indigenous and Black volunteers were initially turned away by many recruiters in Canada. Later, when manpower fell short as ghastly news got back to the home front, they were welcomed in many instances but often segregated into labour corps work. Others sidestepped restrictions if ethnicity didn't come up when they signed up.

Veterans Affairs Canada estimates that more than 4,000 Indigenous men and women served in the First World War. Their website, veterans .gc.ca, estimates the ratio of one in three Indigenous men of service age going off to fight, citing the Algonquins of Pikwàkanagàn First Nation, where just three fit men of service age stayed on reserve. Half the eligible Mi'kmaq and Maliseet men of New Brunswick and Nova Scotia were enlisted, and almost every eligible man from Saskatchewan's File Hills

community went, the site says. In British Columbia's Head of the Lake Band, every single man between twenty and thirty-five volunteered.

In the Air, on the Ground

John Randolph Stacey of Kahnawake, Quebec, was one of four Iroquois officers in Brock's Rangers. He served with the 1st Battalion of the Royal Flying Corps, died in an air accident, and is buried at Heston Cemetery in Britain.

Alfred Clinton Totty, the Métis son of an Anglican missionary and an Indigenous mother in Yukon, served with the 78th Battalion of the Canadian Infantry. He died September 2, 1918, at Drocourt-Quéant from a machine gun bullet to the throat.

Yann Castelnot has devoted years to discovering the extent of Indigenous contributions to the First World War and other wars. His meticulous research carefully cites precise numbers from North American Indigenous communities, from the Abenaki to the Zuni. What he has learned so far about the First World War is that between America, Canada and Newfoundland, there were 16,326 Indigenous people serving. Of those, 1,329 died in service and 1,076 were listed as wounded; there were 2,617 medals awarded, according to Castelnot's website.

The American army provided more opportunity for advancement for Indigenous soldiers than Canada did, Castelnot says, citing one major general, two colonels, three lieutenant colonels, ten majors, forty captains and seventy-two lieutenants.

Among the standouts, William Belmont Newell, a Mohawk man with Penobscot ancestry from Syracuse, was the French interpreter for General Pershing. Leo Maguire, an Osage man, was a captain in the French Army. Roy Lewis, a Cherokee man of Oklahoma, was a mechanic for French aviation.

Yes, in the Great War: Code Talkers

A generation before the famed Navajo Code Talkers helped win the Second World War by confounding Axis efforts to crack messages encoded in their language, Native American languages were used to send coded message in the First World War, Castelnot says.

"The first known use of the tanker code system, under enemy fire, was [by] the Cherokees within the 105th Field Signal Battalion, 30th Infantry Division, serving alongside the British in the Somme," he says. "A German officer captured confessed that his intelligence staff was completely confused by Indian language and did not allow any benefit for the battle."

Castelnot says at least eleven different Nations provided more than 105 code talkers during the First World War, mainly during the Meuse-Argonne offensive in the last two months of the war.

A total of 2,820 of Indigenous soldiers' graves have been identified (including those of veterans who survived the war). If these numbers sound new or unfamiliar, it could be because once incorrect information has been delivered, it's all too easy for it to keep being transmitted wrong, Castelnot says.

"I mostly learned that the so-called official story is not always accurate... Unfortunately, graduate and official writers and historians very often copy what they read or hear and take it for granted, without necessarily checking the words or the data," Castelnot said. "Oral history has the same problem; we repeat the same things over and over, sometimes distorting them according to the political correctness in force."

Washington State to BC to War

One of the names that turns up in Castelnot's research is that of Luke Charles Mahone. The son of Alfred and Emma Mahone of Nitinaht, on the west coast of Vancouver Island, he was the husband of Ethel Mahone of the Coqualeetza Industrial Institute in Sardis, BC. Mahone, a Sardis resident at the time of the war, was actually born in Washington state. He signed up in Vernon, BC. Wounded in the shoulder and abdomen, after four agonizing days he died at the 49th casualty clearing station. His headstone reads: TO THE GLORY OF GOD AND IN TENDER MEMORY.

Most Decorated with Three Military Medals

Sergeant Frank Narcisse Jérome of the Gesgapegiag First Nation in Quebec was one of the most decorated soldiers of the war. The Mi'kmaq soldier was one of just thirty-nine to receive the British Military Medal an astonishing three times over, awarded for his part in battles at Vimy Ridge and Passchendaele.

As the war's bloody toll became widely known, the flow of volunteers was staunched by reports home to devastated families. Earlier, when Canadians began signing up to fight, many Indigenous men were initially turned away from enlistment—only to be subject to the draft in 1917 after conscription became law.

Write the Cost of War in Cree

Fourteen Cree words, etched on the Portland stone tablet that marks the grave of John Chookomolin—dead at age twenty-two—drive home the visceral nature of grief. Their brevity underscores the immeasurable scope of loss. The young man served as 2497978 Private J. Jakomolin in the Canadian Forestry Corps, and died on September 20, 1917. When the stone was replaced because of the need to correct the name, it became the first gravestone in the First World War to use Cree syllabics. According to findagrave.com, the inscription in Cree syllabics reads: "ìKi-na-ka-ta-o Ta-ni-s Ne-s-ta Ni-wi-ka-ma-ka-n Na-meh-ko-si-pi-k O-ma Ma-shi-keh-wi-ni-k O-chiî," which translates to "I left my wife and daughter at Nahmehkoo Seepee (Trout River) for this war."

Rumbling of War: All Ready to Go

Joseph Hookimawillene was a member of Ontario's Cree community. According to Joseph's grandson George Hookimaw, the family name was originally Okimawinnew-Innew, before being anglicized to Hookimawillene, and then shortened to Hookimaw. Joseph came to the war at the end, George said. "According to my uncle, he said it sounded like there was a thunderstorm where they were," Hookimaw

said. "They were ready to go, all packed up and ready to go, and they
heard the war was over."

Brigadier-to-Be from the Six Nations

Oliver Milton Martin was a Mohawk man, one of three hundred res-
idents from the Six Nations of the Grand River who would serve (a
record Great War enlistment for Canadian First Nations). A school-
teacher by profession and part of the 37th Haldimand Rifles militia
regiment of Mohawk men, he enlisted in 1915, according to the website for Library and Archives Canada. An officer with the 114th and
107th battalions, he earned his pilot's wings and survived a gas attack.
Back home after the war, he became a school principal. In the Second
World War, he commanded the Nanaimo (14th) and Prince George
(16th) infantry brigades, finishing his military career as brigadier. He
became a provincial magistrate in Ontario for the regions of York, Hal-
ton, and Peel, according to the Veterans Affairs Canada website, and
was the first Indigenous person to hold a judicial post in Ontario. He
and his wife were invited to the coronation of Queen Elizabeth II.

A Brilliant Reflection of His People

Lieutenant Albert Mountain Horse of the Kainai Nation in Alberta
was the first known Alberta Indigenous volunteer "allowed" to enlist;
he was among the very first Canadians to get to the battlefields of the

Western Front, landing in the Second Battle of Ypres. He was also among the first to be gassed as German forces unleashed chlorine gas, weaponized for the first time, on the Western Front on April 22, 1915, at Saint-Julien. He wrote home: "The Germans are shelling us now. My horse is wounded already. The shells are whistling over our heads. I have been up to the trenches for a long time now. The doctor said he was going to send me to the hospital. I told him I would sooner die like a man in the trenches than have a grave dug for me."

After he was gassed three times, consumption set in. Invalided and broken, bound for Alberta and home, Lieutenant Mountain Horse died on his journey at a military hospital in Quebec.

At his massive funeral, as the *MacLeod Spectator* newspaper of December 2, 1915, recorded, older community members performed a war chant as they joined the funeral procession. Despite a heavy snowfall, the church was at overflow capacity, with both Indigenous and settler attendees together—which was apparently unusual for the time, the paper noted. Town merchants closed their stores and sent wreaths in respect. Archdeacon Tims addressed the Kainai Nation at the funeral in their language, which was reportedly a first for the pulpit in Fort MacLeod. The paper said it was the first time in the known history of that church that a burial service was conducted over an Indigenous person.

Mountain Horse's former schoolmaster, Reverend Sam Middleton
of the St. Paul school, was said to be broken up with loss.

Lieutenant Albert Mountain Horse "cast a brilliant reflection on
the Blood Indians of Alberta," Middleton said at the funeral, calling
him "one of the Empire's greatest sons."

The paper noted Indigenous Chiefs attending his funeral include
Shot Both Sides, Weasel Fat, Running Wolf, One Spot, and Running Antelope. Another southern Alberta hero, Lethbridge's Harry
Watson, was also in attendance. Watson was missing a leg to war
wounds. The last time he had seen Albert Mountain Horse was on
the battlefield.

Lieutenant Mountain Horse's father and three brothers were
among the pallbearers. His belongings were draped on his coffin.
Heartbroken, his weeping mother, Sikski, placed her own traditional
headdress over it. Lieutenant Albert Mountain Horse is buried at the
Old St. Paul Cemetery on the Blood Reserve.

Mike Mountain Horse Elementary School in Lethbridge is named
for Albert's brother, a Lethbridge scout for the North West Mounted
Police who joined up to fight with his brother Joe after Albert died. Joe
was wounded three times; Mike survived being buried alive by a shell
at Cambrai. Upon returning home, Mike Mountain Horse eventually
became a journalist, re-enlisted for the Second World War, and was
elected to the Blood Tribe Council.

Colour Barriers

Who will cut these trees? Build this road? Lay that track? Sling this bridge? Defuse these mines? Move this ammo dump? Battle this explosives fire? Dig that trench? Take away these bodies?

That's the gritty work—the hard, back-breaking work of the labour corps, the "pioneer" toil of war.

The recruiters who turned Black Nova Scotians away from the recruiting stations didn't see their Canadian-ness (which was the same as theirs), just the colour of their skin. However, come 1915, Canadian enlistees "couldn't" be refused on account of race. Some commanders welcomed Black volunteers to stand, fight, and fall at Vimy and Passchendaele with their peers. Others, not so much. In 1915, Lieutenant-Colonel George Fowler of the 104th Battalion showed just how far Canada still had to go in civil rights. He tried to discharge twenty Black soldiers on the basis of their colour: "I have been fortunate to have secured a very fine class of recruits, and I did not think it fair to these men that they should have to mingle with Negroes," he wrote in a huff.

Though discrimination was entrenched (so to speak), the British needed all hands on deck. Some of the most grueling work of the war went unlauded. Often, this unlauded work was delegated to individuals segregated from the fighting soldiers. Construction battalions filled with Indigenous men and Black Canadians laboured at cutting down trees, laying roads and tracks, and slinging bridges. Additionally, labourers brought in from China had unpleasant and dangerous tasks, such as defusing mines, and hauling and burying the dead. The time was ripe for the No. 2 Construction Battalion, CEF. It would be Canada's first, last, and only segregated battalion. Chaplain Captain

Reverend William A. White was the only Black commissioned officer in the CEF, compared to six hundred Black officers in the US forces (still segregated at that time) once America joined the war.

The battalion worked. Six days a week. Ten hours a day. Logging and tracklaying with hand tools in bleak working conditions. Sleeping in segregated tents.

Cut these trees! Build this road! Lay that track! Sling this bridge! Defuse these mines! Move this ammo dump! Battle this explosives fire! Dig that trench! Take away these bodies!

The recruiter will see you now!

The Black battalion's nation would recognize their service late. A 2016 postage stamp hailed the No. 2 Construction Battalion.

Brave is...

Brave is Corporal Freddie Stowers from Sandy Springs, South Carolina, Company C, US 371st Infantry Regiment, seconded to the French army. Brave is what you do on September 28, 1917, rising to lead a platoon in tatters in an actual uphill battle in the Ardennes when your leaders have been gunned down and your troops have been laid to waste. Brave is reorganizing to go forward when the odds stack up hideously against the determined few who remain. When enfilade fire shreds your Plan B, brave leans into machine gun fire because that's how to take the trench. And when you've been hit and your life is ebbing out, much like the war itself, brave is that one final push to forge on. The French Army's Red Hands did take Côte 188 with Stowers's help. He was buried with his peers in the Meuse-Argonne American Cemetery and Memorial.

Stowers's recommendation for the Congressional Medal of Honour was officially "misplaced," remaining unprocessed until Congress asked the Department of the Army to investigate. Finally, some seventy-three years after his death, Stowers's surviving sisters, Georgina Palmer and Mary Bowens, accepted the medal from President George H.W. Bush

and Barbara Bush on April 24, 1991. There is now Stowers Elementary in Fort Benning, Georgia, and Corporal Freddie Stowers Single Soldier Billeting Complex in Fort Jackson, South Carolina, named in his honour.

The Caribbean at War

Often overlooked when contributions are tallied, the Caribbean showed up for the First World War—with 16,000 volunteers. Keith Eastmond of the Ex-Servicemen's Association of Antigua and Barbuda talked with BBC's Gemma Handy. "The Caribbean was keen to support the mother country, as they saw it then. But Britain was reluctant to let West Indian soldiers fight white Europeans in those days," Eastmond said. October 1915 saw the formation of the British West Indies Regiment, with the majority of men hailing from Jamaica, the Bahamas, and British Guyana. For the most part, because of segregation based on skin colour, they were relegated to the tough—and dangerous—Labour

Corps jobs. The BWIR would lose 1,200 men—just 200 in combat, the rest from illness, Handy reported.

Honoured Decades Late

Like many of his fellow Black American soldiers, Sergeant William Henry Johnson was discriminated against in American ranks—but he was accepted quite happily and fully by the French. In the Argonne Forest on May 14, 1918, he suffered from twenty-one wounds in hand-to-hand combat. The Albany, New York, resident fought off the enemy. With grenades. With the butt of his rifle. With a Bolo knife. With bare fists—all he had left. And despite his wounds, he rescued another soldier. All in a day's work for the brave Sergeant William Henry Johnson.

Difficulty in repatriation was widely observed. Back in America, racial tensions boiled over as hundreds of thousands of Black American soldiers returned home after helping win the war. They distinguished themselves at the Western Front, but on the home front they were the targets of racist resentment, which had seethed since long before shifts in wartime population sent Black families to the industrial north for work and to escape segregation. To experience respect in the trench and to return to resentment and racism was no easy thing.

In a story posted online on time.com a hundred years to the day after Armistice, writer Chad Williams notes that while combat in France was over, for Black Americans, another war went on. Williams cites the shattering case of Charles Lewis, one of 380,000 Black American soldiers who served in the Great War. A month after Armistice, Lewis was dragged from his home, jailed, and then seized and lynched by a mob of about a hundred angry, mask-wearing men determined to teach Black people a lesson.

"World War I transformed America and, through the demands of patriotism, brought the nation together in unprecedented ways. But these demands also exposed deep tensions and contradictions, most vividly in regard to race. Black Americans fought a war within the war, as white supremacy proved to be harder to defeat than the German army was," Williams says.

Johnson didn't escape the hatred that was vicious, rampant, and systemic, entrenched at many levels of government. At home in America, he gave speeches that were well-received. He found interest and admiration—until jealousy and discrimination reared their twinned heads over the favourable attention he received in his uniform.

Johnson died destitute in 1929 from untreated tuberculosis.

Honours from his country would be lifetimes away in coming. For the Purple Heart, he would wait sixty-seven years after his death. He would be awarded the Distinguished Service Cross seventy-three years after his death. The Medal of Honor, eighty-six years after his death. Better late than never. Earlier would have been better. The French honoured him without regard to his colour. Sergeant William Henry Johnson was the very first American ever awarded France's Croix de Guerre with Star and Bronzed Palm.

Anyone's War: Muslims Fighting for the Allies

The grave has no favourites; in terms of participants, the First World War was not a "white" war, nor a "Christian" war, nor even a "male" war. It included more than nine million people of varying backgrounds and persuasions.

The Muslim memorial at Verdun (fought from February 21 to December 18, 1916) is dedicated, "Aux soldats Musulmans morts pour la France"—to the 70,000 Muslim Allied soldiers who died at Verdun. The British Royal Legion estimates some 885,000 fought with the Allies in the First World War. "Some 400,000 of them hailed from the British Indian Army, whose 1.5 million troops comprised the largest volunteer force in history," writes Global News national online journalist Rahul Kalvapalle.

A United Kingdom-based project called The Muslim Experience is part of Forgotten Heroes 14-19, a non-profit set up by Luc Ferrier in 2012. A Belgian aeronautics executive, Ferrier believes research shows the actual number of Muslim soldiers who fought for the Allies exceeds 2.5 million—almost three times the BRL estimates, Kalvapalle writes.

Ferrier was inspired by his great-grandfather's war diaries. "I was impressed by the enormous respect he had for his Muslim brothers in arms from all these continents, while he himself was a very devout Christian," Ferrier told the *National*, a UAE-based newspaper, in 2018.

Crossing that River

David Bennes Barkley's Anglo-American father was a career Army man; his mother was Hispanic. Due to his English last name, perhaps, Barkley wasn't shuffled into segregation when he joined up; racism officially demanded that Hispanics and Black Americans were to be segregated from white people in the First World War. After a successful scouting mission into enemy lines days before Armistice, Barkley drowned while swimming back across the Meuse River. He was one of three Texans awarded the US Congressional Medal of Honor, given posthumously. He also was awarded the French Croix de Guerre and Italy's Croce al Merito di Guerra.

He was the second person honoured with having his coffin lie in state in the Alamo. A San Antonio school, a US Army installation, and a Laredo plaza with the tallest flagpole in the United States all bear his name.

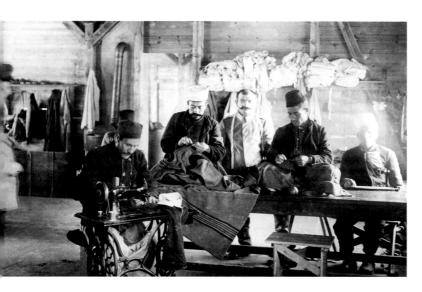

Valour before Citizenship

One of Texas's most decorated First World War soldiers was a Mexican immigrant, and not even a US citizen at the time of his service. Chihuahua-born Marcelino Serna walked across the Rio Grande in search of a better life at age twenty. Menial work was all he could find as he didn't speak English, so that meant working sugar beet crops in Colorado. Rounded up as an illegal immigrant, he was going to be deported, but then he signed up with the US Army's Company B, 355th Infantry of the 89th Division. His military exploits included wounding a German sniper, then following him to his trench and throwing grenades to kill twenty-six enemy soldiers and capture twenty-four, and also sneaking up on a German gunner and taking out the nest, capturing eight. He was wounded in both legs just days before Armistice. Serna was the first Hispanic person to be awarded the Distinguished Service Cross; he also received the Purple Heart with an oak leaf cluster, the French Croix de Guerre with palm and the Médaille Militaire, the Italian Croce al Merito di Guerra, and several others. Serna returned to El Paso, married, and retired as a plumber, living to the ripe old age of ninety-five.

In 2016, the United States named the Customs and Border Protection Port of Entry in Tornillo, Texas, the "Marcelino Serna Port of Entry."

Forgotten Medals

In Vancouver, there is a tranquil greenway memorializing Masumi Mitsui.

Born in Kokura, Japan, Mitsui immigrated to Canada in 1908. He was working as a waiter in the Union Club in Victoria, British Columbia, when the Great War broke out. Racism against Asian immigrants and other "ethnic minorities" in BC meant widespread discrimination. A battalion of 171 volunteers raised by the Canadian Japanese Association was rejected by the Cabinet of Canada. Enlisting in Alberta was less of an issue, so Mitsui went to Calgary to sign with the 10th Battalion of the CEF. He distinguished himself at Vimy Ridge, and led thirty-five Japanese Canadians in the Battle of Hill 70; only five of their number survived. Mitsui ran out at great risk to retrieve a Lewis gun and then used it on the enemy. He earned the prestigious British Military Medal for leadership, bravery in battle, and assistance to the wounded on the battlefield. He was wounded in battle late in April 1917 and was promoted to the rank of sergeant.

Once home after the war, he was an advocate for the suffrage rights of Japanese Canadians. He never supposed his medals would tarnish in the eyes of his country.

Flash forward to December 7, 1941, when the attack on Pearl Harbor brought America into the Second World War with Japan. Mitsui wrote to Canada's minister of national defence on behalf of Japanese Canadian veterans to vow "their unflinching loyalty to Canada as they did in the Last Great War," but as anti-Japanese sentiments boiled over, Japanese Canadians were quickly labelled "enemy aliens" and suspected of spying for the Empire of Japan. The RCMP took Mitsui to register as an enemy alien. Mitsui's family was summarily stripped of their possessions. His chest full of Great War medals—and his offer to re-up—was met with the confiscation of the family's seventeen-acre farm in Coquitlam, BC, which the government sold, giving the Mitsui family a third of its value. Later, the family would dig up a samurai sword that Mitsui's son George had buried. Along with other Japanese Canadians, the family was interned in British Columbia's interior despite Mitsui's decorated service in the First World War. In 1946, interned Japanese Canadians were given the option of repatriation to Japan or relocation east of the Rockies. The Mitsui family moved to Hamilton, Ontario; come Armistice Day each year, he would dress up in his uniform and medals—and stay home.

Much later, as the oldest living Japanese Canadian First World War veteran at age ninety-eight, Mitsui was a guest at the ceremony to relight the lamp on the Japanese Canadian War Memorial in Vancouver's Stanley Park on August 2, 1985. The lamp had been snuffed out in 1942, along with Mitsui's trust that his service meant as much to his country as it did to him. Mitsui stated in an interview: "I've done my last duty to my comrades. They are gone but not forgotten." He died just before his country finally officially apologized to Japanese Canadians for treatment they received during the war.

3

IN THE TRENCHES

Ground Zero: Ypres, Wipers, Ieper

Like a hurricane whose eye has settled on decimating one spot, this small patch of ground at the Western Front absorbed blow after blow, stalled in the place of fury in one ongoing bloody stalemate.

The constant stone in the shoe of the German Imperial Army was the Flemish centre of Ypres. Dubbed "Wipers" by British soldiers (can't imagine Y), Ypres was the world's textile capital in the fourteenth century. The gothic spires of the Cloth Hall, where guilds pitched laces and damasks on the cobbled Flanders streets, would be reduced to a pile of stones—Ground Zero of the key Ypres Salient, her populace evacuated away to safer territory. Half a million men died trying to possess Ypres in three separate battles. Of over 61,000 Canadian men and women who died in the Great War, one in four died defending Ypres from the Germans, who came through but never held it. A huge portrait of Ypres clad in the tatters of destruction adorns the Canadian Senate Chamber today.

The city was restored stone by stone with costly reparations from the German government, wrought from the bowed backs of the German populace. Ypres's destruction was wiped clean of all except for the corrosive resentment that would fuel the re-arming of the humiliated Germany. Today, re-christened Ieper is a town-sized Old World museum. It is exquisite like a snow globe, with a war-torn past, steeping visitors in the sepia tea of history, where shells once brought medieval architecture to her stone knees. The Last Post ceremony glows at Ieper's heart, the Menin Gate, where the names and the ghosts of the ungraved dead cry out for their own reparations for stolen years.

First Gassed at Kitcheners' Wood: They Held the Ground

The Fighting 10th Canadian Battalion and the 16th Canadian Scottish Battalion were among those decimated in a nightmarish nighttime counterattack in the Second Battle of Ypres at Kitcheners' Wood on April 22, 1915, after being ordered to seal the French line broken following the first-ever chlorine gas attack. A fresh creeping hell, a green horseman of a new apocalypse, emerged at Kitcheners' Wood; evil genies from tanks of chlorine slunk across No Man's Land, uncoiling at the enemy's bidding, wafting on the breeze. It sank in the Allied trenches, killing—and teaching how to kill. It shocked even the Germans unleashing it. Hanging back, reluctant to advance through the fumes lest their newfangled masks fail, they failed to fully seize the chlorinated moment.

The stench of chlorine filled the nostrils of the unsuspecting men, so sharp in their throats and eyes as to be beyond bearing, closely followed by genuine suffocation and pain behind the sternum. Each fast breath became a small bomb, each cough the Grand Canyon. Retching with furred tongues, their knees buckled—and recline could be fatal as the heavy fumes clustered at ground level. As the bronchial catastrophe was unleashed, they lapsed into delirium and sleep and death.

All was not fair in war. Friends fell, not to wake again, faces green-yellow, sicking up blood-streaked vomit and then lapsing into lethal sleep as bronchitis stole in and fever rattled brains into delirium. Seventy-five per cent losses devastated the troops. Forging on despite bad odds and ill planning in the first offensive operation by the Canadian Corps on Belgian soil, they were later awarded unique acorn and oak leaf titles, worn on the shoulder. On the advice of Lieutenant-Colonel George Gallie Nasmith and Dr. Francis Scrimger of the 2nd Canadian Field Ambulance, the order was passed to use urine on handkerchiefs for makeshift gas masks. (Eventually troops were issued gas masks, and the Allied side used gas on the German side in return. By Armistice, 100,000 tons of gas had killed 40,000 troops.)

"It was the steadfastness of the Canadians, who refused to recoil before the lethal gas, and the promptness and dash with which their reserves came forward that closed the road to Calais. The stand they made was one of the most gallant and courageous deeds in the history of war, and the advance of their reserves was a magnificent sight that will never be forgotten by those who witnessed it," writes Edward Morrison in his memoir, discovered in a shoebox by author and editor Susan Raby-Dunne, who turned it into *Morrison: The Long-Lost Memoir of Canada's Artillery Commander in the Great War.*

They stayed there, but the casualties were enormous, Belgian battlefield guide Raoul Saesen told me on a 2016 tour, pointing at two wreaths, new and bright, swathed in purple ribbons and dedicated to the Canadian Scottish Regiment (Princess Mary's) and the Calgary Highlanders—and the memorial itself is to the 10th and 16th Battalions.

"The good news was that Ypres remained in Allied hands a second time. The bad news—the losses and the use of chlorine gas... But they held the ground, they held the ground. Everyone agrees if they wouldn't have been there after the first usage of gas, the Germans would have broken through... If Kitcheners' Wood had been taken, in no time the Germans would have reached Ypres square. The action prevented the Germans from breaking through beyond Ypres."

The veterans of Kitcheners' Wood were permitted to wear a unique shoulder badge, an oak leaf with acorns. On April 22, St. Julien's Day,

Louis Raemaekers

the Calgary Highlanders still toast with glasses held high: "The Glorious Memory of the 22nd of April, 1915!"

A Rare Place at the Front: Poperinge

Hops for that Belgian beer were probably sprouted in Poperinge, called Pop for short. In the Great War, Pop was one of the rare places to get a good night's sleep, one of just two towns in Belgium not under German occupation. Seven miles away from Ypres, it was a safe place to billet British troops and for field hospitals. A statue designed by Nele Boudry recalls Eliane "Ginger" Cossey, a charming girl who worked at La Poupee Café. Pop was an R&R getaway for the war-weary (Talbot House, dubbed the "everyman's club") and an elegant oasis, then and now, a shelter eschewing rank or class. You can still get a hospitable cuppa there amid the loveliness of cobbled streets. Nearby at Lijssenthoek cemetery, thousands of soldiers sleep forever.

Lijssenthoek: Where Names Match Bones

At Lijssenthoek, it was a sort of Publishers Clearing House in reverse: someone would knock on a citizen's door and inform the occupant that their house was needed. At the farm named Remi Quaghebeur, a widow was told: "We need your farm for a hospital in just the right place. Close to the Front, but out of range of shells." Instead of carrots and turnips, they planted surgeons and thousands of hospital beds and sowed bodies. At this hospital graveyard, unlike battle-side graveyards across the Front, the dead are almost all identified. Just thirty-five out of 10,786 burials are unidentified with the bones of former patients that lie beneath them. The memorial fence of metal pickets mark the days like a calendar for the lifetime of the hospital at Lijssenthoek, Belgium. Notches tally how many were buried each day as the wounded continued to flow in from advanced dressing stations and the clearing station. At Lijssenthoek, the names match the bones.

Veiled in Shadow: Vancouver Corner

At Vancouver Corner at Saint-Julien in Langemark, Belgium, First World War veteran Frederick Chapman Clemesha's statue, *The Brooding Soldier*, stands on Canadian soil with Canadian shrubs on officially Canadian territory. Chiselled from a 10.5-metre shaft of granite, he stands where 18,000 Canadians withstood the first German gas attacks. He seems to bear the weight of the war on stone shoulders; cloaked in art deco rock, he personifies grief and anger simmering. When applying for the contract for the creation of the monument, Clemesha wrote: "For our part, we do not wish to brag or glorify militarism. To a citizen soldier, and to the parents of the 50,000 who did not return, the thought of achievement and victory cannot be disassociated from the thought of sacrifice."

At Vancouver Corner, a plaque recalls Kamloops, BC, engineer and machine gun officer Lieutenant Edward Donald Bellew. With his troops destroyed and the enemy less than a hundred yards away, harbouring no hope of reinforcements, he duked it out until his ammunition failed. Then he seized a rifle, smashed the machine gun so the enemy couldn't use it, and fought to the last before being taken prisoner on April 24, 1915. In 1919, after his release from four years in a German POW camp, Bellew discovered he was the first Canadian awarded the Victoria Cross.

Birth of a Poem and a Legend: Essex Farm

Ontario-born Lieutenant-Colonel John McCrae was destined for poetic immortality for words scribbled during a break from his gruesome job in a tiny hospital bunker at Essex Farm on the Western Front in Flanders on May 3, 1915. Days turned to months, seasons, and years. The doctors in the trenches couldn't stop the flow of men, of bodies, of guns, of pain, of war. The crosses continued to pile up, row on row, unstaunched and undeterred by explosions, unfailing in their return.

McCrae was depleted from battlefield medical practice, from tending to the victims of the April 22, 1915 gas attacks at nearby Kitcheners' Wood; he was bone weary from triaging in the advanced dressing station near the Front—another ambulance, another casualty. McCrae thought of Lieutenant Alexis Helmer, a friend and former student newly lost at the Second Battle of Ypres, and he wrote what would be immortalized:

> In Flanders fields the poppies blow
> Between the crosses, row on row,
> > That mark our place; and in the sky
> > The larks, still bravely singing, fly
> Scarce heard amid the guns below.
>
> We are the Dead. Short days ago
> We lived, felt dawn, saw sunset glow,
> > Loved and were loved, and now we lie
> > > In Flanders fields.

Today, pilgrims bent on a quest to know of the war of their forebears seek the station at Essex Farm out in the ghostly remains of the advanced dressing station, makeshift clinic, and morgue a stone's throw from the German trench. The ceiling is sunken under the weight of a century's wars and fragmented pieces of peace and poppies.

In a dirty bunker, sheltered by earth and strewn with small commemorative poppy-clustered crosses, modern visitors to nearby Kitcheners' Wood can see where McCrae made the brutal choices he faced as a doctor triaging on the Western Front: We can save this one. We can help that one. We can ease the pain for these ones. We can send home the effects of those ones. No identification on that one. We can't do anything for that one.

Although McCrae succumbed to pneumonia in France in 1918, his poem "In Flanders Fields" is referenced by millions every year come Remembrance Day. A hundred years later, the larks still bravely sing and fly. All's never silent from guns somewhere on this globe, but Lieutenant-Colonel John McCrae's words live on long after him.

Mad about *Lusitania*

On May 7, 1915, the deaths of hundreds of civilians after the sinking of the luxury ocean passenger liner *Lusitania* enraged American sentiments. The handsome luxury ocean liner cradled so many mysteries. A torpedo from a German U-boat and an unexplained inner explosion sank her off the Irish coast.

There are many tales buried in Great War graveyards. Leland Wingate Fernald's headstone tells but one: the New Hampshire painter signed up November 11, 1915, in Esquimalt, BC, to be a driver with the 5th Brigade Canadian Field Artillery while his country was still trying to keep out of the war. He died of shrapnel wounds to the head. A VOLUNTEER FROM THE USA TO AVENGE THE LUSITANIA MURDER is engraved on his Portland stone marker at Lijssenthoek.

For *Lusitania* and her passengers, Fernald made it his war long before his country did, dying a year and a day later at Lijssenthoek hospital. The sinking of the *Lusitania* was one of a number of reasons cited for the US eventually joining the war in the spring of 1917, although its status as a civilian liner has long been debated. Many Americans took Fernald's cue and went before their country did. More than 35,000 soldiers in the CEF listed their birthplace as the US or Alaska. When the US entered in April 1917, they did so with decisive force—and at great loss. In the remaining year and a half of the war, from a country of ninety-two million, there were more than 116,000 American military deaths (almost double the Canadian death toll for the whole war) and almost twice as many wounded. Today, the National WWI Museum and Memorial in Kansas City ranks as a top American museum, and tells the stories of America in the First World War.

From New York City to the Front

Born in New York City, Alexander Matier enlisted in the US Army and served in Cuba in the Spanish–American War. In 1915, he was one of thousands of Americans to enlist with the Canadian Expeditionary Force to avenge the sinking of the passenger liner *Lusitania*.

He wrote in a January 1918 letter that he was nearly captured by the Germans at Hooge near Ypres. Matier and his mates were holding the old German first-line trenches, establishing posts. He was stationed four days in a mine crater covered with the dead bodies of Germans.

"You could not turn a spade of earth without uncovering a body; we were standing in water up to our hips, in which were dead bodies, on which we were compelled to walk, as a moment's exposure meant certain death as the neighbourhood was covered by snipers," Matier

wrote. In the dugout where they rested, human limbs were sticking out of the wall under layers of mud and sandbags and terror, and in the trench, the stench was terrible, he said.

"What is commonly called a birdcage had been erected by the Germans, and in this they had their snipers who could see without being seen. It was a regular death trap, and we had been given to understand we had a small chance of coming out alive. We were attacked the first night in, but the men in this post were mostly daredevils, we met them halfway, and surprised them, I think we used about sixty hand grenades on them," Matier wrote.

Badly wounded in the leg in Belgium, Matier spent two years convalescing before his September 1918 discharge. He didn't live much longer, dying in Winnipeg, Manitoba, in 1920.

Immigrant Home to Stay

You can go home again—but you might have to stay. Migration from Europe to North America was reversed by the war for some. There was Richard Verhaeghe. Born in Ostend, Belgium, he enlisted with his new country to save his old country. Lance Corporal with the infantry in the 5th Canadian Mounted Rifles (Quebec Regiment), he was honoured for his work in the grim battle for the Regina Trench (the longest German trench of the war). On October 2, 1916, "he stayed behind in the open and dressed wounded, being all the time under extremely heavy fire, rifle and machine gun fire, without any regard for his own safety... He succeeded in getting several of the wounded into their own trench," the citation read.

But there was no time to enjoy the honours. Lance Corporal Verhaeghe was killed in action on October 30, 1917, at age thirty-nine—just forty-eight kilometres from where he was born. He is the only Belgian Canadian known to be buried at Tyne Cot Cemetery in Belgium.

How to Bury a Man at Sea

For some soldiers, the war meant world travel to places like Africa, India, the Persian Gulf, especially when the war went truly global in its scope in 1917—but it was anything but glamorous, despite the promises of see-the-world recruiting posters.

Allen Matheson Conquergood was at the older end of the age spectrum for regular soldiers. At forty-five, he had a good twenty-five years on many of the fellows he marched with. In 1914, recruiters were picky, turning away many potential recruits: Uses eyeglasses! Flat feet! Too short! Too light! Too old! By the time the Kincardine, Ontario, local was enlisted in 1916 with the 239th Battalion's Railway Construction

Corps, recruiters could no longer be so discriminating. In fact, Conquergood's medical records show he was missing fingers on his right hand from an agricultural accident. The doctor concluded he could still write and seemed to do okay. He passed with points to spare.

At war, Conquergood wrote lengthy journal entries. He wrote about the harrowing time when he was in a boat stuck on a sandbar in a river near Baghdad, where he was to build a bridge in the Persian Gulf where other boats had been destroyed. He described deadly fires on board his ship and explosions in the coal bunkers. He wrote about the fierce heat and the hundreds of camels and donkeys that helped with work on the Khur River. "Bridge completed. I had quite an adventure today, I killed a big wolf with a tent pole, he was very bold, for he came right into camp, he was as big as a timber wolf."

Amid awful weather, tragedy struck a seasick man, Conquergood wrote. "Storm still ragin'... One of the soldiers heaved last night till he burst a blood vessel and died, so we had a funeral this morning... They sew people dying at sea up in a canvas and weight it with iron and wrap the flag around the canvas loosely, put the corpse on a plank, slow up and stop the boat, hold the flag and tip up the plank and they slide off into the water, but first... a short service."

Stark conditions sometimes led to madness, he noted.

"June 22... Last night a couple of men went off their head. One came to me and woke me up and told me I had several bad wounds but that he had fixed them up and I would soon be alright again, but he was determined to set down on top of me. Of course I moved," Conquergood wrote. "About then the guards came and took him to the hospital. It is very warm, and I think the heat brings these things on."

On the Trail of Five Bronze Caribou

At the time of the Great War, Newfoundland and Labrador was not a Canadian province. Its contribution as a separate British dominion was disproportionately large. Some thirty-five per cent of men between the ages of nineteen and thirty-five served by 1918. More than 6,200 served with the Newfoundland Regiment.

Newfoundlanders also served forestry, naval, and military units. Famed for their sailing, Newfoundlanders filled the colony's naval reserve with two thousand sailors and fishermen. Others served on Allied military and merchant ships; of five hundred known merchant sailors, one in five died.

After brutal casualty rates caused volunteer rates to plummet, compulsory service became law in April 1918 in Newfoundland, as it had in Canada in the fall of 1917. Support or the lack of it divided on largely religious and eco-political lines.

Canada Day to the rest of the country, July 1 is now Memorial Day in Newfoundland and Labrador. They were the only North American regiment in the bloody fray near Beaumont-Hamel, on the opening day

of the Somme offensive, July 1, 1916. There were 710 killed, wounded, or missing out of 801 present in a thirty-minute attack on German positions. That was a lot of grief for one rock.

Cast bronze tablets were placed with the support of the women of Newfoundland, the mothers and sweethearts and sisters and aunties—a lot of money was raised to make sure the lads were properly acknowledged, their names already seared on their families' hearts. It was a cost almost too great to be borne: the abomination that is grandsons survived by their grandmothers.

Heroic Even in Death

A galibot (child miner) from age thirteen in the Béthune, France, pit mine, Corporal Fernand Marche of the French 130th Infantry

Regiment volunteered for a dangerous job. He emerged from a shell hole bearing the critical message: at all costs, the brigade needed to know the regiments had been cut off. They were in danger. So was the battle's outcome. Reinforcements were desperately needed for the regiments. Husband to Angelina Louisa Maria and father of two precious children, Marche ran with valour.

Shell fire wounded him mortally that August 1, 1916, but that couldn't quench his resolve. In death's steely grip, Corporal Marche crawled to the path. He hoisted the message wallet high. If he had to die, then as life ebbed, he would still do his best. Soon his breath was gone, and rigour mortis set in, but the liaison spied the wallet in Marche's lifeless hand, raised high from his fallen body. The Front and the battle's outcome were secured by Marche's valour, even in his death.

Regret to Inform

A teacher in Edmonton, Eugene Robert Drader was born in London, Ontario. On September 12, 1916, he wrote to his parents, "All our troops are very optimistic these days. We have the Huns on the run all over. We all expect to be home soon."

Four days later, he was killed in action with the 49th Battalion. He was twenty-five. Upon his death, his best friend, Lieutenant Harry E. Balfour, wrote a letter to the Draders.

"This is without doubt the hardest task I have ever had to do— telling you of the death of your son and my best friend... Two days before we went into action I had transferred to 'D' Company to be with Eugene, little thinking that our long and intimate friendship was to end so suddenly and so tragically... He was buried near where he fell—a real soldier's burial, not the parade style of military funeral, but the short hesitating prayer that was said over his grave, with our heads bowed very low on account of machine gun fire, the most sincere prayer ever offered up... He was the best friend I ever had... Since his death I am not the same; I cannot be; but everyone is kind and I have received much kind sympathy, for we were known as inseparables... As deeply as I feel it, it can be nothing in comparison with your feelings... I wish you knew the excellent influence he has had on the lives of the young who knew him as their teacher. They worship him, and what is more, they try to imitate him. Many, many hearts in Edmonton and Gull Lake will be very, very sad... It seemed at first that

no one could be more heartbroken than I myself; and I took chances for over a day in the front line that I never would have taken otherwise; I seemed to be obsessed with the one idea, that Eugene and I must not be separated. But I know there's nothing to compare with father's and mother's love, so I send you sympathy and I mean it more than I ever meant those words before... I share your sorrow, words cannot say how deeply. Yours with sincerest sympathy, Harry Balfour."

Awful Somme

Serving with the 19th Battalion, 6th Infantry Brigade, 2nd Canadian Division, George Morton Bird of Port Alberni, British Columbia, wrote to his father on September 28, 1916, describing the German barrage at the Somme as "awful."

"A machine gun bullet went through my helmet and grazed my head, and also pieces of my helmet or bullet hit me in the shoulder. I laid in a shell hole for about ten seconds and decided to go on, when I saw I wasn't badly hurt. As it turned out I did the best thing I could have done as Fritz shelled us fierce and the wounded out behind us got hit very bad," Bird wrote.

"J. Thomson and Cole from Port Alberni were both killed, I believe, though I can't be quite certain. It certainly is hell, but I think Fritz (the Germans) gets it far worse than we do. We had two or three prisoners (wounded) come out with us. You should have seen them duck when one of their shells came over when we were coming out. The shell fire and machine gun fire we had to go through is impossible to describe. The whole country around there is simply blasted to pieces... I suppose I shouldn't tell you this but I know it will go no further than you know in safe, and I wanted you to know where I had been in case anything should chance to happen in the future which God being willing I don't think will," he continued.

Bird was killed in France on May 6, 1917, in the Battle of Arras.

The Whole Side Wall Had Come Out

William Lowry immigrated to Prince George, British Columbia from Britain before the war, then enlisted to go back and fight for his first country. In an October 4, 1917, letter he expressed horror at the barbarities at the Front: "Trench warfare is so hideous that I will not harrow you with any description of it. I have been in action . . . at Ypres Salient . . . and on the Somme, where our battalion 'went over' and took Regina Trench. What renders the fighting so appalling is the artillery fire. On the Somme it is continuous, day and night, world without end. The sacred historian of the Deluge wrote that 'the windows of Heaven were opened.' Had he been recording the Battle of the Somme he would have said that the whole side wall had come out!"

Walking Wounded

Getting treatment could be something of an obstacle course for the walking wounded. George Hedley Kempling of Toronto journaled his experience in the fall of 1916. A German shell struck the roof of a dugout where he was tending to some stretcher cases.

"It bashed the roof in and drove a beam down on my head, forced my front teeth out a bit and splintered all the front ones," Kempling wrote.

"After I had recovered myself, I ran out to a nearby dugout with three comrades, all of us dazed . . . we went back and helped get the stretcher cases back 1.5 miles to our battalion doctor's dugout at the bottom of a shell hole and then thirty feet under the ground. While

sitting there in the dugout, trying to eat something, though I had no appetite, I collapsed and cried like a baby."

Kempling had hoped to tough it out.

"I want to stay and help our brave stretcher-bearers out with the rest of the gallant fellows who were lying out in the front line, wounded, but a day, a night, and a day with nothing to eat, fighting or working continuously, with no sleep and at last this crack on the head did me ... So I went out with three other walking cases. We managed to walk overland, dodging German whiz-bangs all the time to the advanced dressing station five miles farther back," he wrote.

Out of the four battalions of the 4th Brigade of 3,000 men, Kempling said, there were not over 250 left that fall.

For George Kempling's grandson, Jim Kempling of Victoria, BC, his grandfather's memoirs led to a PhD in history at the University of Victoria and a website (acitygoestowar.ca) about Canadian cities in the First World War.

"He kept notes every day that he was overseas ... after he died, I got his diary," Jim Kempling said.

After his severe concussion while serving in the artillery, George Kempling went to England to convalesce; from there he was sent back to France to join the Forestry and Railway Corps. He ended up running YMCA centres behind the lines before returning to Canada.

Leave the Light On

When he'd play rugby, Lieutenant Eric "Puss" McLeod Milroy's mother used to tell him to stay unhurt, to play "well back" in hopes that he wouldn't get injured. An accountant with a master's degree and an international rugby player with the Black Watch, Milroy wrote his mother: "We are in some slight trouble tomorrow. So I am just warning you there is to be no 'keeping well back' then." Five scant days later he was killed at Delville Wood on July 18, 1916, at the Somme. He is honoured on the Thiepval memorial to the missing dead. In maternal denial, Margaret Walteria Milroy never fully believed her son was dead. She left a light on in his room, hoping he'd come home and find his way up the path. No soldier's parent could blame her for such magical thinking.

A Rugby Players Memorial was dedicated in 2017 on the Chemin des Dames Battlefields at "Rugby Players Trench." There on September 16, 1917, fifteen international troops who played the game together perished together. John Dennison is an ex-rugby player and official who organizes commemorative sporting events and memorials. He and Franck Viltart from the Conseil départemental de l'Aisne launched the World Rugby Memorial Project in October 2015 at the World Rugby Museum at Twickenham Stadium. A monument designed by former French rugby captain Jean-Pierre Rives was unveiled at Craonnelle in 2017. Of Eric Milroy, Dennison said: "A man who was a born leader, and always at the centre of the action, Milroy, like many rugby players of his time, came through private education, and when enlisting was made an officer. There are many examples of these men who were killed in World War I, with them leading from the Front."

Hockey Hall of Famers

Four Hockey Hall of Famers paid the ultimate price in the First World War, according to Alan Livingstone MacLeod. He is the author of *From*

Rinks to Regiments, which details thirty-two largely forgotten men of the Hockey Hall of Fame who served in the Great War.

Lieutenant Frank McGee of Ottawa lost the use of his left eye as a young hockey player, but that didn't stop him from being a leading scorer for his team in the Stanley Cup playoffs just after the turn of the twentieth century. He signed up with the CEF in 1914, enlisting with the 21st Infantry Battalion. He was wounded when his armoured car was blown into the ditch by a high-explosive shell, but months after his knee was damaged, he sidestepped the opportunity to work at headquarters and headed back to the Front. On September 16, 1916, at the Somme, he was one of 298 whose bodies were never recovered or identified. His name is engraved on the memorial at Vimy Ridge, along with 11,000 others lost in France with no known grave. McGee was one of the first eleven enshrined at the Hockey Hall of Fame, MacLeod writes.

Scoring three goals a game in his hockey career, George Taylor Richardson was an exceptional hockey player and known as a gentleman on the ice. At war, he was an exceptional leader. Well-heeled from a prominent Kingston family, Richardson used his own money to ensure men in his command in the 2nd Battalion had warm boots, gas masks, and cigarettes; he even provided for their families in his will. He died from sniper fire when he went out past the Canadian lines to lead his men back to safety. "No officer was ever more beloved by his men, who were willing to follow him everywhere," a fellow officer was quoted in the *Toronto Star*, MacLeod writes.

Eight-time Stanley Cup winner and Toronto Maple Leafs coach, manager, and owner Constantine Falkland Cary Smythe is better known to hockey fans by his hockey name, Conn Smythe. He enlisted

with the Canadian Field Artillery, serving from 1915 to 1919. He was awarded the Military Cross for "conspicuous gallantry" and leading his men "with great dash" at the Somme, where he resisted the German counterattack, rescuing wounded compatriots and killing three enemy soldiers. He asked to be reassigned to the Royal Flying Corps, where he learned to fly under Canadian ace William Barker, the most decorated Canadian serviceman, who would later become the first president of the NHL's Toronto Maple Leafs—of which Smythe was part owner. Smythe was shot down and spent the balance of the war a prisoner of war in Upper Silesia, according to *From Rinks to Regiments*.

Front Fare

Decent drinking water at one particular post was a serious issue as the farm pump was located beside the manure pit, wrote Charles Henry Savage. Civilians drank beer or wine; a regimental water wagon brought chlorinated drinking water from elsewhere.

"At first we got bread only once in two or three days and then not much of it, while vegetables were almost an unknown thing. There was however plenty of hard tack, bully beef, cheese, and in our particular unit, apricot jam: four articles that became so hard to get towards the end of the war that they were considered delicacies. I don't know where all the cheese came from, but literally tons of it were wasted," he said. "We had more and larger slices of cheese than of bread, and a common and very tasty snack before turning in at night often consisted of a large slice of cheese thickly spread with apricot jam."

Cases of bully beef and hard tack were sometimes just used for dugout flooring, Savage said.

Food scarcity was a reality at the Front, where supply lines could be severed for days by heavy fighting. One hungry Canadian soldier, David McLean, wrote home that gifts of socks and underwear weren't as essential as food that could be hoarded or shared—or devoured by hungry soldiers. "Don't put anything in that you can't eat. Other things are useless," he wrote. You wouldn't have to read too closely between the terse lines to understand they were going hungry.

Making light of food scarcity sometimes helped; George Vowel talked about digging a kitchen behind the trench. "Of all the concoctions that was ever cooked up, we have them all skinned enough to give the devil indigestion. We take turns cooking fancy dishes you will never see at any of the swell hotels. Yesterday we had Mulligan stew hobo-style with whatever anyone could find. Made it with hard tack, bully beef, oatmeal, dates, yes, together. We call it 'Give and Take.' You take it because there's nothing else; it gives you a belly ache ... Set a spell; a sign above the door reads 'You are welcome—a refuge for the sick, lame, and lazy.' First here, first served is our motto. Today I braved brambles and snipers for blackberries for dessert. We'll have a bite mixed up for Fritzy if he ever comes over."

Making Christmas merry wasn't easy on the Western Front, but efforts were made, according to a letter home from Robert Shortreed, written as a heavy snow blanketed the ugliness of the Front. The

Guelph, Ontario, man described the surroundings and the mid-war decay to his sister.

"Wood is more plentiful here and we can get all we want out of the ruins of houses just outside our door. Any buildings that still stand have their walls punctured with shell holes," he said. "One thing, this place is full of rats, and some of them are larger than most cats or at least look it."

Chicken was served at the holiday dinner, and an allowance of plum pudding per soldier. "The chicken could have been younger," he said.

Festive food aside, there was no holiday truce by that year—such fraternizations were strictly banned by higher-ups on both sides. The treats felt at odds with the artillery fire in the near distance. "It seems hard to be throwing shells at one another on Xmas Day but I suppose they cannot stop the war even for the day," Shortreed said.

Little Brown Jug

Soldiers were actually dosed with rum from stoneware jugs, morning and night, as if it were medicine. There was plenty of controversy on the home front and in some leadership circles over the use of what was clearly a crutch for men on the brink of death at all times.

Harold Henry Simpson of Bayview, PEI, wrote to his mother that it was hard for those who hadn't been in the war and under those conditions to understand the need for such things.

"But when one takes the infantry man in the front line waiting to go over the top, standing cold and wet with the mud halfway to his knees, and knowing exactly that at the end of a few minutes he will be called upon to face the most fiendish and effective instruments of destruction that modern science has been able to invent, from the fifteen-inch shell to the Mills bomb, from liquid fire to gas, one cannot help thinking that a shot of rum, which for the meantime makes them feel warm even if in reality they are not any warmer, and which for a time makes them forget in part the horrors they have to face, is a good thing for them," Simpson wrote just before the Battle of Vimy Ridge on April 9.

In a letter home, Laurence Earl Johns of Elimville, ON, said he drank good tea three times a day. The drinking water by itself wasn't much good.

"A person cannot say that he drinks rum. You do not get a drink, only a swallow. It will strangle you quicker than white wine vinegar if you go to take a breath between the two little swallows while your wind has gone for the time being," Johns wrote. "But it cheers one up wonderfully after being up all night with nothing to eat to see the sergeant coming up the trench with the rum in a water bottle under his arm. We are always willing to wait a few minutes longer to get our issue. If you ever hear anybody say that they think it's a shame that the soldiers are given rum, why just tell them a thing or two from me. I'll bet they don't have any boys over here. They don't know under what conditions we have to live over here." Johns died on September 12, 1917.

Careful in his consumption, George Hedley Kempling promised his sweetheart to be temperate.

"This morning we were wakened up for a ration of rum. Of course as per promise to Gussie I passed it by as I was not in necessity. The

"Excuse me! You're standing in my shaving water."

rum is really an emergency ration served out when the men are wet or extra tired, or after an engagement or a heavy shelling when nerves are badly shaken," he journaled.

Those who returned were often expected to be able to "handle" their liquor. The dependence deemed so essential for making it through the war would prove crippling for many after Armistice.

Wartime Humour

How would the joke go, again? "A German, an Austro-Hungarian, a Belgian, a Serbian, a Frenchman, a Briton, a Canadian, a South African, an American, an Italian, a Caribbean, a Russian, a Japanese, a Chinese, an Indian, a Thai, an Australian, and an [insert nationality here] all walk into a war..." A natural response to stress for some, humour cheered and relieved tension at the Front. It was seen as a morale builder in a grim era. (Lice were a common source of humour.) Comedy shows were brought to places like the Talbot House in Poperinge, Belgium, where soldiers let off steam.

Those seeking to reassure family and friends at the home front sprinkled letters with jokes. In August 1915, Walter Robus took a break from his dangerous work on the bomb squad to draft a letter to Reverend Arthur Mansell Irwin, pastor of the Norwood Methodist Church in Norwood, Ontario. "We have tea and mud for breakfast, skilly and mud for dinner, and tea and mud for supper. Who wouldn't be a soldier?" he quipped. (Robus resisted all offers to return home, despite repeated injuries, so maybe he was onto something.)

Major Reverend William Beattie was minister at the Presbyterian Church in Cobourg, Ontario. He enlisted and became senior chaplain to the 2nd Division. Beattie's letters were often laced with humour, and published in the *Cobourg World* newspaper.

"I heard a good louse story yesterday. A Tommy found a louse in his moustache. He picked it off and holding it up said, 'What a deserter, eh, go back to the barracks!' So saying he opened his shirt and tucked it in."

Kidding aside, Beattie described for his readers the difficult conditions faced by the troops. "In the trench, about a foot or two from the bottom, there is a step against the parapet on which men stand to fire. Along this lay, sound asleep, many of the poor fellows. It was raining and they were vainly trying to cover both head and feet with the rubber sheet."

Beattie was made a Commander of St. Michael and St. George for "his most conspicuous gallantry and distinguished conduct at the gas attack at Saint-Julien and through all the subsequent severe fighting of the period. Working unremittingly, with complete disregard to danger, he assisted in collecting wounded on many fields of action." He returned to Ottawa in 1918 to organize the Chaplain Service of Canada and was promoted to the rank of colonel.

4

WOMEN'S WORK

War was a two-edged sword for the women of the post-Edwardian era. Most of the eligible men left for the Front. That left war work and regular jobs literally "unmanned." Women who in previous lives stayed close to home with young families or traditionally "acceptable" jobs suddenly had the opportunity to engage in other occupations. They had reason to, as well: times were tight with breadwinners gone. Recruiters got innovative as they looked for women to do regular jobs normally reserved for men, as well as war work. Picking up the labour slack in "great opportunities!" was deemed "freeing men to fight!"

"Needed—50 skilled female stenos—American Army QC Corps!"

"Adventure in France! Seeking phone operators for army switchboards near Front—parlez French SVP!"

"Queen Mary's Army Auxiliary Corps in France: cook, fix, file or miscellaneous!"

"Farm Service Corps—just-for-now help needed!"

"Women replace men gone to Front!"

Elizabeth Foxwell, author of *In Their Own Words: American Women in World War I*, writes about individual women and their roles in the war at elizabethfoxwell.com.

"It's heartening to learn of these women's achievements in WWI despite obstacles, yet troubling to learn about stories of discrimination, to learn about promising lives and ambitions cut short, and—most disturbing of all—to learn about such women lying in unmarked graves with little or no evidence that they received or are receiving suitable recognition for their service," she says.

Foxwell has theories on why US women's service in the First World War is often ignored. There may have been less coverage of women from lower income or societal brackets—and less attention paid overall to women's history, she speculates.

Women genuinely wanting to help in war efforts may have not wanted to be perceived as hogging the limelight, either.

"Some women felt they were just doing their patriotic duty and thus deserved no acclaim, or that their stories were less important than those of the men doing the fighting and the dying," Foxwell says.

It's inspiring to learn of women triumphing over barriers, she says, citing the example of female physicians who were rejected from the Army Medical Corps and told they could be accepted only if they went as nurses. "They found support through the National American Woman Suffrage Association, organized and sent all-female medical units to Europe, performed heroic service, and were decorated."

She has heard from people proud of their relatives' service in the war, and others who are simply interested in learning more about women's involvement in the war effort.

"Some stories I've uncovered have been poignant, such as that of Jennie Cuthbert Brouillard, who obviously had experienced PTSD and stated in an oral history, 'After I come [*sic*] home, I couldn't nurse anymore ... I was just all worked up inside,'" Foxwell says.

Women achievers in science during the Great War stand out not only for their accomplishments, but also for their rarity. STEM careers were often reserved for men, while women were most likely to find a role in nursing, a profession they could more safely pursue within traditional Western society's roles.

Rosie the Riveter of Her Day

On the home front, not all jobs were "appropriate" and safe. The "Rosie the Riveter" of her era, Lottie Meade glowed in her war-work jumpsuit, with her beautiful attitude and a hand on her hip. She was a mother of four, self-confident, proud to do her bit for home front service. She performed "essential" work with hazardous munitions—and it was essential, as eighty per cent of the munitions for the Allies were made by women, according to Forces.net. It meant better wages than working in a shop, and she earned the title "Munitionette," working long hours and six-day weeks to keep those explosives heading for the Front. Working with explosives was more risky than working in a

1st

Munitions worker
Lottie Meade

shop, too: Munitions plants had improper ventilation and poor working conditions. Toxic chemicals meant yellowed skin, which led to the workers being nicknamed "Canaries"—and, for Lottie, death by TNT poisoning. Literally the canary in the coalmine, she brought attention to the workers' plight. A UK Royal Mail stamp in 2016 remembered Lottie Meade a century after her death.

The Only English Woman Soldier

An orphan with a dream, the original stunt journalist was forbidden to cover the war because she was a woman. Dorothy Lawrence wondered what it would take for a woman to get into the British Army. With the help of what she called her "ten khaki accomplices," she donned a male persona, complete with straight-razored face and a shoe polish tan to cover her fair skin. She wore a tight corset to conceal her curves, cotton batting to pad her shoulders. She did her homework; absent the months of training others received, Lawrence took clandestine lessons on drilling and marching.

She slipped onto the Front, passing as Private Denis Smith of the Leicestershire Regiment for ten days in the summer of 1915. Worried about keeping up the ruse when she got sick, she turned herself in, and reportedly was ordered by the War Office not to publish. Her eventual book, *Sapper Dorothy Lawrence: The Only English Woman Soldier*, was an international hit, but heavily censored. Her life was not an easy one before, during, or after her odyssey at the Front. Lawrence confided to a doctor that she was raped by her church guardian as a girl. After the war, after the book, she was deemed insane and committed to an asylum where she died decades later, only to be buried in an unmarked pauper's grave—but not before breaking new ground as a female journalist under deep cover.

In His Place

Some were meant to be soldiers, and some weren't. That's what Milunka Savić thought, so she pretended to be her brother. When the Serbian army called the lad up, she went in his place, disguised as him—the original *Hunger Games* with a Great War twist. Alas, her gender was uncovered, literally, when she was wounded and a doctor prepared to treat her. Savić asked to return to the field; her commanding officer, annoyed perhaps that a woman had walked in men's ranks in stealth, said he'd answer her "tomorrow."

"I'll wait," she said. Not budging. Just waiting. Rifle straight. Embodying guts and chill.

After an hour of her standing there (how unnerving was that?) her commanding officer grudgingly agreed she could stay in the army. Good call. The odds were "ever in her favour." Milunka Savić went on to become the most decorated female fighter in the history of warfare, period. In 1916, she captured twenty-three Bulgarian soldiers by herself. Hers are the French Légion d'honneur (twice), the Cross of St. George, the Most Distinguished Order of St. Michael (English) and the Serbian Miloš Obilić Medal. She was also the only female recipient of the Croix de Guerre (French) with the palm attribute. After a brief marriage and having a child, she went on two adopt two orphans. For the icing on the cake, in the Second World War, she was invited to attend a prestigious dinner with occupying Nazis. She refused. For that she earned ten months in jail. Milunka Savić lived a long life, dying at age eighty-one. There's a street in Belgrade named for her.

A Stamp for Her

A British woman who liked to drive, to adventure, to rebel, Captain Flora Sandes did life on her own terms. Nursing was the way to be part of the war, as combat was verboten for women. Sandes formed the Women's Sick and Wounded Convoy Corps to help out with the war effort. Through a fortuitous mix-up while working for St. John Ambulance in Serbia—and for safety as well as to get food rations— she enrolled in the Serbian army. She made leadership strides she never could have dreamed of in the British forces as a woman. With

Британске хероине Првог светског рата у Србији

74

Флора Сендс (1876–1956)

Serbia

ПОШТА

СРБИЈА

М.КАЛЕЗИЋ   2015   ФОРУМ

pluck and skill, she rose quickly through the ranks to sergeant major.
Wounded by a grenade in hand-to-hand combat in 1916, she earned the
highest decoration of the Serbian military: the Karađorđe Star. Also in
1916, she wrote a memoir, *An English Woman-Sergeant in the Serbian
Army*. She then ran a hospital and raised funds for the Serbian Army.
After demobilization in 1922, Flora Sandes lectured extensively around
the world, and published a second memoir. She returned to England
after being interned (with her husband) by the Nazis in 1941. In 2009, a
street in Belgrade was named for her. She was honoured with a Serbian
stamp designed by Marina Kalezić, one of a series of six honouring
British women for their humanitarian work in the First World War.

Nobel Winner and X-Rays

In her young adult book, *Women Heroes of World War I*, author Kathryn J. Atwood looks at "16 remarkable resisters, spies, and medics." Among them, a young Marie Curie. The two-time Nobel Prize recipient for groundbreaking work in chemistry and physics, Curie was the mother of more than a million X-ray diagnoses. She brought the technology someone else invented to battle zones in the form of mobile X-ray equipment called "petit Curies" to search for shrapnel and bullets inside the wounded. "She pressed through the many bureaucratic obstacles placed in her way," Atwood writes. (Other medical advances at the Front included direct blood transfusions, one soldier to another.)

Atwood says she wanted to bring to life an era not fully captured by early film technique.

"Everything was black and white, people walked herky-jerky, and what was the war about anyway?" she says.

She found illumination in the form of *Downton Abbey*, the hit television series whose second season opens on the eve of the First World War.

"Oh, my goodness, these were real people," Atwood says. The women who could be most involved in the front lines of the war effort were those of more independent financial means, she says.

"The women not of means couldn't go because they had to stay home and work, but the new woman was on the rise. What that translated into was these women who had means to go and didn't need to stay home and work could go off and have an adventure."

As a writer, she seeks stories with a narrative arc that can keep young people interested in reading, Atwood says. That, she found in spades in her Great War research.

"They wanted to do what they could do. There was a sense of excitement almost universally; it was almost like the Olympics—they were going to make their mark for their country. There was nationalism and patriotism, and a pride in serving. Poor men could go, but rich women could go, too," Atwood says. "I was looking for just the right opening quotes, as if these people were speaking to us from a hundred years ago. Instead of just a book about the people, the people themselves got to say something."

She was fascinated by the Russian Battalion of Death, a formidable group of Russian women soldiers formed in 1917 who fought ferociously on the side of the Allies.

"The Russian provisional government was desperate to stay in the war. These women actually wanted to fight, wanted to take their part," Atwood says. In addition to their desire to fight was the ambition to shame young Russian men reluctant to become battlefront fodder in a war that killed their countrymen by the millions. The idea behind the RBD was, "If these women can fight, why can't you?"

Nurses at the Forefront

The recruitment line went something like this: Nurse—See the world! Your nation needs you! France, Belgium, Home front CEF! Adventure! Duty!

The American Red Cross recruited 22,000 nurses for the US Army during the war, and half of these tended wounded near the Western Front. The US Navy had an additional 1,500 nurses. Some 3,000 Canadian nurses served overseas in the First World War—"bluebirds," they were nicknamed, because of their uniforms.

Kindness bloomed in angst-filled rooms, amid bedpans, thermometers, needles and urinals, sheets and scalpels, midnight watches, fevered brows, broken bones, shattered nerves, damaged lungs, blood, sweat, and tears. Despite all that, in war's deep gloom, kindness thrived. Humour unfolded in an autograph book, like paper poppies from grateful wounded soldiers where battle loomed ... and kindness bloomed.

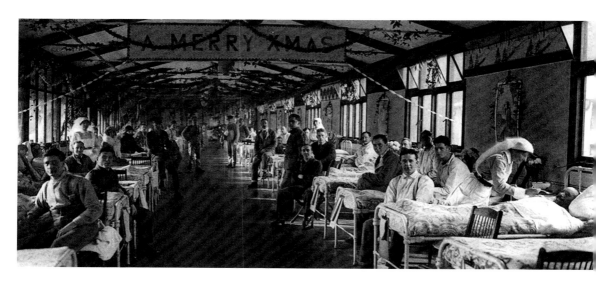

Leading in Research

Author Elizabeth Foxwell cited groundbreaking nurse Marie X. Long of York, Pennsylvania, as the first female lab assistant at Camp Greene's base hospital in North Carolina. Noted in the *Caduceus* in August, 1918, Long had trained three years in lab analysis and worked at the US Army Hospital in Lakewood, New York.

She went on to publish scientific articles like "The Value of the Wasserman Reaction in Diagnosing and Treating Syphilis." (*The American Journal of Nursing*, Vol. 21, No. 6, Mar., 1921, pp. 369–375.)

A modest biographical note in her papers at her alma mater, Hanover College, tells us Indiana-born Rachel Emilie Hoffstadt developed an oral vaccine for typhoid while serving as head bacteriologist in the hospital lab at Camp Sevier, South Carolina. Foxwell reported that Hoffstadt was also an instructor of chemistry and bacteriology at the Army Nurses School. She was the groundbreaking first female graduate of Hanover College to earn a doctorate—and she earned two, one from the University of Chicago and one from Johns Hopkins University.

Fundamentally a Pacifist

Charlotte Edith Anderson Monture was undeterred when she couldn't get nursing training in Canada because of her Indigenous status. She travelled from her home on the Six Nations reserve in Ohsweken, near Brantford, ON, to America, where she graduated at the top of her class at New York's New Rochelle Nursing School. Because of *Indian Act* restrictions, it was difficult for Indigenous people to pursue higher education as they could be stricken off the band register if they were deemed to be "enfranchised," her grandson John Moses told me in January 2020. Additionally, her applications to Canadian nursing schools were arbitrarily rejected without even the courtesy of an interview, he said. "Her way around that was to take nursing training in New Rochelle … she then volunteered to serve as a nurse with the Army Nurse Corps with the American Expeditionary Force," Moses said. It's believed that although twelve Indigenous nurses served overseas, just one of them, Monture, was of Canadian extraction.

While serving at Buffalo Base Hospital 23 in Vittel, France, she formed a friendship with one of her patients, a young Iowa soldier who had been wounded in the neck. He was believed to be in recovery, so when he died of a sudden hemorrhage, Monture was deeply saddened. "It upset her," said Moses. "She wrote to his parents, and told them he wasn't alone." When the fellow's parents made a pilgrimage to France in the 1920s, they came to visit his last nurse on the way back, and they kept an ongoing friendship, Moses said.

Once the previous *Indian Act* restrictions were removed, Monture returned to the Six Nations Reserve, where she raised her family and continued her nursing career. She became the first Indigenous woman to vote in a Canadian federal election, thanks to legislation that enabled Canadians who served to vote, regardless of gender or background. Her daughter, Helen Monture Moses, became one of the founding members of the National Aboriginal Nurses Association. Edith Monture, as Charlotte was known, had a long and interesting nursing career, including service as a leader in the Red Cross in Ontario.

Monture died in April 1996, just shy of her 106th birthday. John Moses recalled his grandmother as a determined person who was also a churchgoer. "By temperament to begin with, she was fundamentally a pacifist, and a very kind person," he said.

Patriotism Is Not Enough

A pioneer of modern nursing methods, the British nurse Edith Cavell treated the wounded of both sides in German-occupied Belgium, helping two hundred Commonwealth soldiers escape. Arrested, she reportedly said she did it and that she wouldn't stop helping them. Death by an executioner's bullet for Cavell on October 12, 1915, sent shockwaves around the world, sparking long debates about the rules of war. Her words are inscribed near Trafalgar Square: "Patriotism is not enough; I must have no hatred or bitterness towards anyone." Cavell's death at the hands of the German firing squad was one of a number of reasons often cited for the United States joining the First World War. The Church of England Calendar of Saints commemorates her annually on October 12. In 1916, Mount Fitzhugh in Jasper National Park was renamed Mount Edith Cavell.

Air Raid Claims

Near the end of the war, Nursing Sister Gladys Mary Maud Wake was stationed near the front lines, where the wounded were—and where the battle raged nigh. Wake, thirty-four, was far away from the Class of 1912 at Royal Jubilee nursing school and her hometown of Esquimalt, BC. She died May 21, 1918, of wounds received in an air raid near the 1st Canadian General Hospital in Étaples, Pas-de-Calais, France.

Full Military Honours

Nursing was the main avenue open to women seeking to help with the war effort at the Front. Staff nurse Nellie Spindler enlisted with the Queen Alexandra's Imperial Military Nursing Service. She expertly treated urgent abdominal chest and thigh wounds at the No. 44 clearing station at Brandhoek. It was seven miles from the front lines—but

not out of range of German shells aiming for munitions. Spindler knew they were all in danger, but her letters home to England were full of cheer. She never saw the exploding shell that sent a large piece of shrapnel through her back. Her nurse's watch stilled forever on August 21, 1917. On the casualty form for officers, she was listed as killed in action. She was one of just two women in one of the largest Commonwealth graveyards; she was buried at Lijssenthoek with full military honours and the Last Post. The Director of Medical Services of the Army and the Surgeon General attended her funeral. Her grave is one of the most decorated and visited of all the thousands of graves at the Lijssenthoek cemetery, overflowing with poppies and crosses laid by awed visitors.

Talent for the Troops

When Black American troops in Europe were treated to classical piano concertos by Helen Eugenia Hagan after the war in 1919, they enjoyed a dazzling talent. Part prodigy, part pioneer, Hagan was a composer who had played the church organ at Dixwell Avenue Congregational Church in New Haven, Connecticut, at the tender age of nine. She went on to become the first Black woman to graduate from Yale University. A composer—although all but one of her works have been lost—Hagan had a career as a college professor at Bishop College in Marshall, Texas, before her death in 1964.

All that together made it more puzzling that her New Haven grave was unmarked. That really got to Virginia author Elizabeth Foxwell, who led a successful crowdfunding campaign to place a marker on what was an undistinguished grave for such a distinguished woman. In 2016, the crowdfunded monument was unveiled by New Haven mayor Toni Harp.

Who Put the Poppy on Your Lapel?

Why do some of us walk around with a poppy on our lapels come the beginning of each November? The story of the friendly little poppy is, in large part, the story of Madame Anna A. Guérin.

Once a skilled lecturer for Alliance Française, Guérin became a brilliant fundraiser around the Western Hemisphere for the war effort and for France in recovery after the war left the country in tatters. She was known to some as "the greatest of all the war speakers."

"She had an enviable, dynamic presence—she could canvass areas just recently canvassed by others and bring in thousands more dollars," says Heather Johnson on her website, a British writer who has made Madame Guérin the centre of her work.

John McCrae's famed poem "In Flanders Fields" first brought attention to the modest little wildflower that bloomed out of the upheaved earth torn by war.

"Madame Guérin was there to work her magic with the symbolic bloom and take the poem's sentiments further," Johnson said.

As early as 1915, Poppy Days sprang up to raise funds for infirmaries, and for widows and orphans.

In September 1920, the American Legion adopted the poppy as a remembrance emblem after Madame Guérin spoke about her "Inter-Allied Poppy Day" idea at their convention, and within a few years many groups and countries went for poppies in a big way.

"Canada was the first Empire country to adopt the poppy, and it set an important precedent for all other Empire countries to follow," Johnson said. "For all her US Poppy Days and Drives afterwards, Anna would visit a town, hold a lecture, and enlist the help of local women. Women and girls were the backbone of her campaigns."

Other poppy influencers included US-born Moïna Belle Michael and Mrs. Mary Hanecy of Milwaukee.

"For me, the French woman Madame Anna A. Guérin is the most significant personality. She saw the potential of the poppy emblem to help her belle France and those who had survived the First World War, alongside the remembrance of those who had lost their lives in it. What singles her out is the fact that her dynamic personality drove forward the campaign... where she led, so many others followed," Johnson says.

5

NOT WANTING TO FIGHT

Baby Talk: Conscientious Objectors

The voracious war monster must have bodies. As stories drifted back to the home front about the grim realities of the Great War, more widows "don weeds," which means to wear mourning black. More telegrams cause households to go dark with mourning. There are voluntary enlistment flags, and turns into the draft. Those who resist volunteering are shamed with white feathers, called out in public meetings. Conscientious objectors, publicly mocked as unmanly, are called anything *but* conscientious, imagined as a ridiculous cartoon created for a Wimereux nurse's autograph book by an injured soldier with his artistic streak intact. See the "snowflake" of his day. Shiny patent dress boots! An eiderdown quilt in his blanket roll! A baby soother close at hand! A hot water bottle nearby! Tea and sweets and insect powder ever handy in pockets!

Handfuls of men were exempted for religion: Quakers, Mennonites, Doukhobors. Some were exempted for critical occupations like farming—someone has to grow food for the troops. Some resisted the call to arms in light of horrific casualty rates. The absence of a uniform frequently brought shaming, delivery of a white feather, hostilities, mocking, and bullying from some whose husbands and brothers and sons were at the Front. Those who willingly fought were pressured to scorn those who wouldn't. The degree of resistance sometimes determined the official treatment. Many were subject to brutality, hard labour, and prison. Some stood in harm's way, treating the wounded on front lines with the Friends' Ambulance, operated by Quakers who refused to raise arms; others grimly concluded that as medics, they were still enabling war.

Make Me: Propaganda

And early flurry of enlistment stalled mid-war. The questions loomed large for recruiters: How to get men to fight when the word was out on war's brutality and carnage, told in blood-bathed forests and never-ending lists of those killed in action, missing in action, or dead of wounds—not to mention poison gas? How could family men and students be lured from their warm, cozy homes in St. Catharines to head straight for the decimation of a generation? What might induce them to pick up a bayonet and really use it (there's no using a bayonet halfway)? Rumours of Hun savagery helped. Propaganda was a powerful tool—a rumour spiralled into an unprovable legend and jagged art of a Canadian crucified on a barn door.

In his book, *Private Peat*, Private Harold R. Peat claimed "the Germans caught and crucified three of our Canadian sergeants. I did not see them crucify the men, although I saw one of the dead bodies after," he wrote. "I was told that one of the sergeants was still alive when taken down, and before he died he gasped out to his saviours that when the Germans were raising him to be crucified, they muttered savagely in perfect English, 'If we did not frighten you before, this time we will.'" The book was adapted into a film in which Peat played himself; the movie was used for recruitment.

Posters printed by the tens of thousands called for new recruits, appealing to everything from pride to ethnic roots—Irish, French, British—to bolster flagging enlistment. What happened in Belgium could happen here, they were warned. Your Motherland won't forget you, said a poster illustrated with a beautiful woman draped in a flag, in a close embrace with a Canadian soldier.

Another poster showed drowning civilian victims from the sinking of the ship HMHS *Llandovery Castle*. Ultimately, it was peer pressure that really applied the thumbscrews. The women were pressured to pressure their men and their sons. An American recruiting poster portrayed a lovely, proud American mama offering up her son to the altar of war's sacrifice: "America—here's my boy," it read. A bounty went out for new recruits. Shame and positive appeal to manhood and ego were the most powerful motivators of all. A recruiting poster from the recruitment office in St. Catharine's, Ontario, urged men to "Be British!" "Play the man!" It offered "comradeship and protection of men from your own city." If all else failed, there was an appeal to their pride and desire for visual status. "The latest and best style of clothes is khaki! Get it on and show your manhood!"

Dedicated to University of British Columbia students overseas, the *UBC Annual* opened with a note from the editor that the journal "comes into being at a time when stirring deeds are the order of the day; a time so momentous that never before, during all the history of the ages, has the world been called upon to face so grave a crisis; when all the carefully-built-up fabric of Christianity seems to be tottering to its fall, under the scourge of the most ruthless and sanguinary people that the world has ever known; whose deeds of brutal savagery make

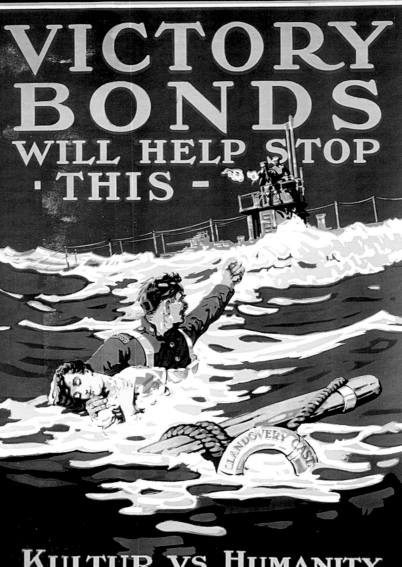

the atrocities of their barbarian ancestor, Attila, seem mild by comparison, and even eclipse the mad-cap antics of Nero, 'The Fiddler,' whose deeds have long been regarded as the highwater-mark of human depravity.

"At such a time as this we naturally ask ourselves the question, 'What is the University of British Columbia doing as its share in helping to save the world from this threatened catastrophe?' Loud and high the answer comes, 'On the blood-red fields of France and Belgium, on the desert wastes of Mesopotamia, on the rocky shores of Gallipoli and Salonika, even on the Eastern Front, in the realm of the Great Bear, are the men who formed the first classes of this University, cheerfully laying down their lives in defence of the sacred cause they hold so dear, and although the UBC is the youngest University in Canada, not one can show a more splendid record ... We have indeed reason to be proud of our men at the Front, some of them merely boys in years, yet who in the thick of bloodiest onslaughts, and in the midst of the most damnable of shell fires, coolly and carefully gave back shot for shot, and opposed bayonet to bayonet, so manfully that the 'fiery Hun' would much sooner attack anywhere else than on the Canadian lines."

A leaflet encouraged neighbours to rat each other out: "Give us his name! His name is ___ His business address ____ His house address ____ His occupation ___ Come on! You know ONE man who won't face his chums when they return from the Front, who is living snugly and safely at home while YOUR loved ones are fighting his battles for him. All we ask is: give us his name. He'll get his chance, now, to PLAY THE MAN! (This help comes from a (MAN) or a (WOMAN). Indicate your sex when sending this card. 255th QOR Overseas Battalion."

Shot at Dawn

A Shot at Dawn Memorial at the National Memorial Arboretum in Staffordshire, UK was modelled after seventeen-year-old Private Herbert Burden, a volunteer who was shot for desertion. Designed by sculptor Andy deComyn, the sculpture shows young Burden blindfolded, with his hands tied behind him, facing the firing squad. Around him, there is an eerie assemblage of stakes, one for each of the 309 Commonwealth soldiers (boys, some of them, as young as fourteen) who were Shot At Dawn. There were twenty-five Canadians among them, ordered to be executed by their superiors. Crimes ranged from abandoning their post, running toward home, leaving the battle or putting down a gun to leaving the trench to warm up or sleeping on the job after days awake—sometimes short on food—in vigilance and terror. (Yes, in addition to more obvious felonies, these were considered crimes.) The terms used were desertion, cowardice. Since every man was essential, an example must be made, the higher-ups decreed. 309 examples, all told. The acronym for Shot At Dawn is SAD. And they were.

In the preface of his book, *Remembered in Bronze and Stone: Canada's Great War Memorial Statuary*, Alan Livingstone MacLeod recalls time spent as an eighteen-year-old helping his great-uncle clean up an old house on Cape Breton. The stories of the First World War that veteran Harrison Livingstone shared with him linger still.

"Memories of another platoon comrade who had 'gone sweet' on a French girl and went AWOL to follow his bliss. Court-martialed for desertion, the friend was sentenced to be shot at dawn. Harrison was

assigned the duty of standing guard over his comrade on the last night, warned that in the unhappy event of a prisoner escape, Harrison himself could look forward to facing a firing squad. Bad as that role was, there was one worse: at dawn, a firing squad selected entirely from his own platoon took their positions and ushered their comrade to kingdom come. The friend, sixteen at the time of his enlistment, was an old hand of nineteen on his final morning," MacLeod writes.

Typically, the accused had no legal representation (after all, they reasoned, this was a time of war). And certainly no military honours. There would be no proper marker, no pension for a grieving wife. The problem, which they might have seen coming, was that in retrospect, most desertions could be attributed to PTSD, combat stress, medical illness—or even a hearing disorder that caused vertigo that made standing to attention and hoisting a rifle impossible. So the executions—in hindsight—were barbaric, at least to some. Others from military traditions maintain the Shot At Dawns were an expected and necessary wartime routine. The heartbreaking compounding of it meant families were shamed (think of Mrs. Patmore on *Downton Abbey* with her SAD nephew). Then there were mothers with no husbands, no pensions; fatherless children would be taunted as the coward's kids.

Execution Squad

Added to the shock of the Shot At Dawn situation, soldiers and officers were forced to shoot their fellows. "It was a sort of target practice and guard of honour combined," writes Kenneth Walter Foster in his memoir of the war. A British man who emigrated to Victoria, BC, he served on an execution squad of one of the twenty-five Canadian soldiers shot at dawn. "The officer in charge politely informed us that the following morning at dawn we were to act in the capacity of an official firing party when one of our own men was to be shot for desertion. He was court-martialed on two previous occasions and was let off on some pretext or other. The third time he met his doom and the execution was carried out in this manner."

The prisoner, a man of about thirty-five, was placed in a chair, tied and blindfolded, with a piece of paper pinned over his heart. The rifles, previously loaded with half live rounds and half blanks, were placed on the ground about thirty feet away. The firing party them marched into the old farmyard. No verbal command was given; the party acted on the blast of the officer's whistle.

"We were first reminded that failure to carry out instructions would mean the same fate … As I remember it, the whole thing only took about a minute … It is with some effort that I recall the facts that transpired on that eventful August morning. Not being murderously inclined … it was some time before I could get the disagreeable subject off my mind. Such is war. The ways of mankind are strange. At war, the penalty for not killing is death; in peace, the penalty for killing is death," Foster mused.

There were holdouts to the shot-at-dawn system: Australia and the US refused to execute their "disgraced" soldiers.

Pardons came much later. In 2000, the Canadian Parliament put the names of their twenty-five executed soldiers on the Roll of Honour. Succeeding generations are left to wonder which will linger longer, their memories or the national shame that they were killed by their own side.

Belgian photographer Geerhard Joos has captured the Vimy Memorial in every possible light, visually chronicling families who lost more than one son to the First World War. But his specialty is the SADs, and he has travelled the world to capture their headstones. "I felt a lot of these guys were done a great injustice … So my sense of justice told me to treat them with equal respect, and I take their photos as well," he told me.

Talk This Out

Julia Grace Wales saw the problem of war this way: once blood is shed, there's no going back.

So the Canadian-born English literature professor at the University of Wisconsin came up with the Wisconsin Plan. A die-hard pacifist, the Quebecer concluded the fix was continuous mediation by smart people from neutral countries, who listen to delegates from "belligerent" countries, in an effort to mediate an end to the barbarities of war. Keep listening. Keep talking until it's done. The great-granddaughter of the first paper mill owner in Canada, Wales brought the plan to the table as part of Henry Ford's anti-war expedition to Europe. Her idea wasn't a bad strategy for life, or for war for that matter, and US President Woodrow Wilson seemed to like Wales's scheme. But there was the German U-boat sinking of the civilian luxury liners *Lusitania* and *Llandovery Castle*—and then the secret but inflammatory Zimmermann Telegram. American public opinion—and congressional ire—was roused. The US entered the Great War in 1917, shortly after the Ford expedition. Ultimately, the infusion of America's four-million-strong manpower (and firepower) helped end the war within a year and a half. It came with a cost: the Americans lost more than 116,000 in that protracted war.

6

1917 AND 1918

April 1917: America Joins the Frayed

The new year of 1917 started with a match to a powder keg for the United States. The Zimmermann Telegram, a botched German effort to form secret alliances, brought the wrath of America down on Germany. Thanks to a cracked code and slashed transatlantic cables handicapping German behind-the-scenes schemes, the not-so-secret secret Zimmermann Telegram was a bombshell. The German Foreign Office clumsily proposed a clandestine military alliance between Germany and Mexico. The offer: If the US were to enter the Great War against Germany and were to lose, Mexico would get the spoils of war in North America for siding with Germany and aiding in her victory. Specifically, Mexico could take back the long-American border states of Texas, Arizona, and New Mexico, lost seven decades earlier in the Mexican–American war, as the spoils of war if they joined the German team. This offer, revealed to the US through secret spy channels in plain diplomatic sight, infuriated US officials and helped propel America into the war, sealing Germany's fate. Mexico stayed out of it.

▲ *American troops at Camp Dix prepare for war.* US GOVERNMENT ARCHIVES

The US had other beefs, too—still smarting from the sinking of passenger liners, escalated reports of German atrocities, and even the distant but shocking death of nurse Edith Cavell. The last straw (in addition to the telegram) was the German navy taking the gloves off for all-out supremacy of the Atlantic, which would endanger not only America's traffic but also her economy. On December 7, 1917, America declared war on Austria-Hungary. In this war, at least, they would never declare war on anybody else—Bulgaria or other co-belligerents, for example. By tailoring their aggression, they would not have to send soldiers to fight in far-off places like the Middle East, the Caucasus, Africa, Asia, the Pacific, or even Eastern Europe.

Explaining all this to the public and to Congress was, perhaps, a bit uncomfortable for President Woodrow Wilson. But there was nothing half-hearted about four million troops.

Over There

According the United States Library of Congress, on April 6, 1917, composer George M. Cohan had two inspirations for his wildly popular

song "Over There": a three-note bugle call, and (most notably) hammer headlines shouting that President Woodrow Wilson had abandoned America's stand-off stance. America was at war. The catchy song borrowed verse material from a nineteenth-century ditty, "Johnny Get Your Gun." Singer Nora Bayes recorded it at 78 RPM for the Victor Talking Machine Company on July 13, 1917. Woodrow Wilson called it "a genuine inspiration to all-American manhood." The sheet music went super-platinum, with multiple millions sold by the end of the war. "And we won't come back until it's over over there!" Only, even when it was over over there, it wasn't over over there. The song itself would outlast the fractious peace of the Treaty of Versailles, and would eventually be resurrected for an anthem in the Second World War.

While the cheery songs of the day were intended to keep up morale in the trenches, for some soldiers laden with an unnamed post-war misery that would generations later be called post-traumatic stress disorder, and the families missing loved ones who would never make it back to the home front, the zippy tunes would start to cloy. "Pack Up the Troubles in Your Old Kit-Bag (and smile, smile, smile)." Because "It's a Long Way to Tipperary" and you will resent being down on the farm "After You've Seen Paree" (if you make it home at all). "When

Johnny Comes Marching Home" (if you can still march then), we'll "Keep The Homefires Burning" (the house down). Four years of fighting, from somewhere in the middle of North America to board ship, to Salisbury, England to train in the shadow of Stonehenge. To Ypres, to Arras, to Cologne. To hell and back, and then to home. From charming and witty to brusque and withdrawn. From clever repartee to stone-faced to sullen to morose to bellowing. They couldn't imagine what made him so difficult to live with. Was it because they couldn't imagine? According to the Canadian War Museum's website, "the crying, fear, paralysis, or insanity of soldiers exposed to the stress and horror of the trenches was often held by medical professionals to be the result of physical damage to the brain by the shock of exploding shells. Military authorities often saw its symptoms as expressions of cowardice or lack of moral character."

Unforgettable

"Not an easy thing, not a thing you soon forget," writes Maurice Bracewell in his memoir. Bracewell, who enlisted in Vancouver in 1915, describes finding friends "lying there face up in all manner of grotesque shapes." He was watching Fritz blow up coal mines when his partner suddenly crumpled, falling at his feet. "Shot over the heart by a sniper." He recalls hearing the shells whistling overhead on Easter Monday morning, watching "the barrage-curtain falls turning the whole of Vimy Ridge into one exploding hell." Not a thing you soon forget.

Bracewell fought at Vimy Ridge, and at Passchendaele, where he was wounded. He returned to Vancouver and became a teacher.

Death Penny

Bill Irving of Ucluelet, British Columbia, has his uncle's "death penny," a bronze cast penny, like a large medal, with his uncle's date of death. Bill has been to his uncle's grave at Vimy Ridge, and has taken his wife and now-grown children to pay their respects to Uncle Roger. It's a quiet, well-tended place, the place that broke his grandmother's heart. Young Private Roger Irving's job was to pop up and signal back, in semaphore, to the artillery. Pop up, signal back, wave those semaphore flags to the artillery, and hunker back down to safety. A dangerous job, even for a lightning-fast seventeen-year-old. A job with a low survival rate. Sure enough, a sniper's bullet gored his pocket journal, literally piercing his father's hopes for his son, found in the inscription: "From your father with wishes for a speedy return and season's greetings." Forever a teen at Vimy Ridge, so very young, he did what his country asked of him. Roger Irving scarcely had time to write in his journal, although he wrote "Sept. 5—sig section" and "trench mortar." Under white stone he rests amid thousands in a wheat field at Vimy Ridge where immaculate graves are tended daily, tenderly, with thanks, a flower at every marker.

Take This Ring: A Will at the Front

Soldiers enlisted for "the duration of the war," which many people underestimated in their optimism. A British soldier might hop a ferry across the English Channel to go home on leave, but Canadian, American, and Indian lads who signed up in 1914 might not see their homes across vast oceans for four or five years. Upon enlistment, soldiers made out "military wills" that basically left their effects to next of kin in the event of their death. Occasionally, with a critical battle looming, they made trench wills and last bequests. Pictou, Nova Scotia-born and Saskatoon resident George R. Chisholm made out a rough-hewn note just before dying at Vimy Ridge. Chisholm's last will and testament was simple: France, April 6, 1917: "Please return the enclosed ring (carbuncle) and Gillette razor to my next of kin. George R. Chisholm. G.R. Chisholm, ___ Ave. N., Saskatoon, Sask., Canada."

Finishing the Journal

Sometimes soldiers ran out of pages and had to scrounge for more paper, but sometimes the notes were just dates and places, following their progress. And sometimes they halted abruptly, heartbreakingly. One tender diary was kept by James A. Jones of Richdale and Calgary, Alberta. Jones wrote frankly, from the heart, chronicling his faith, his love—and he voiced his misgivings. In 1917, he wrote with a sense of foreboding and impending doom that was, as it turned out, well-placed:

> "Thursday, April 26, 1917—Front line, Heavy shell fire, terrible experience. Too bad this thing must continue."
>
> "Friday, April 27, 1917—In support of dugout, brick yard Fritz dropping heavies over on top of us. Appear to be in danger of death all the time."
>
> "Sunday, April 29, 1917—Day opens quietly. 1st, 2nd and 3rd Divisions have gone over the top. Our turn next. Lord help us."
>
> "Friday, May 4, 1917—Got three lovely letters from Fannie. I am glad I have such a good wife, God grant I may be spared to return to her again."
>
> "Friday, May 11, 1917—Relieved ten o'clock at night. [I got] lost and spent night in bush under shell fire."

"Friday, May 18, 1917—Sports in afternoon. Feel blue as I think of return to trenches. I want to see the dear old home again."

"Wednesday, May 23, 1917—Our last day in Reserve. Wonder if I will live to come out again. 'War is hell,' said General Sherman, and I wonder what would be his thoughts if he could see this one."

"Saturday, June 2, 1917—In supports and due to go over the top on Sunday morning. This may be my last entry if among those who fall. I die firm in the belief of a crucified Christ. I want my wife to know that my only regret was on her account, and I die blessing her with my last breath. May God protect her."

When his things were returned to her, Fanny Jones made the final, touching notation in James A. Jones's journal, with underlines:

"Friday, June 29, 1917—The day my darling died. Gone but never forgotten," she wrote.

In 1917, the student committee of the University of British Columbia dedicated the school's first ever annual to their alumni and fellow students overseas who went off to war, "in recognition of the sacrifice made by those of our comrades 'who took the khaki and the gun instead of cap and gown.'"

"University men of British Columbia, we rise to salute you, for your deeds have helped to make British Columbia's 'Iron Brigade' famous in a nation famed for its regiments and their glorious traditions," read a note to "Medallists." A roster of over a hundred students on active service is accompanied by the names of twenty wounded, and eight who died, complete with year they had expected to graduate.

The editor said the school's Canadian Officers Training Corps was one of the finest in the Dominion, and cited UBC's course in gas engineering, "in this, the most technical and scientific of wars."

Alberta Olympian

When Alexander Wuttunee DeCoteau was training near Stonehenge, King George V gave him his gold pocket watch for winning a five-mile race at Salisbury. DeCoteau, of the Red Pheasant Cree Nation, fought with the 49th Battalion, CEF in France. A Cree Canadian and the sole Albertan at the Stockholm Olympic Games in 1912, he took eighth place for Canada in the 5,000 metres. He was Canada's first Indigenous police officer, joining the Edmonton police force in 1911.

DeCoteau signed up for the CEF in 1915. He was thinking about mortality when he penned a letter home on September 10, 1917, to his dear sister. He said he was lying on the ground, trying to finish his letter before dark. "I hope I do, for I don't know when I'll have another opportunity," he said.

It would be his last letter home.

"A man has lots of time to think of his people and home out here, and one does get awfully lonesome at times. I know in my last trip to the front line, I dreamed of home and 'all the mothers, sisters and sweethearts' I ever had... Most of the boys... believe that everything is prearranged by Divine Power, and if it one's time to die, no matter what one does, one has to die. Their motto is, 'If my turn comes next, I can't do anything to avoid it, so I should not worry.' They don't worry, either. Of course there are lots who suffer from shell shock or nervous breakdown, and they can't fight against fear, but most of the boys have a keen sense of humour, and laugh at almost anything..."

Fleet of foot, DeCoteau had run messages and guided troops through danger for two years to the Second Battle of Passchendaele. There, he was felled by the bullet of a German sniper on October 30, 1917. He was buried among six hundred other Canadians on the Bellevue Spur. In 1985, members of the Cree community performed a ceremony in Edmonton to bring his spirit home to rest on the prairies. The memory of his short life lives on at several sports halls of fame, and at a park named for him in Edmonton. A residential area in south Edmonton was named for him in 2014.

Inuit Hero on Thin Ice

John Shiwak was one of a handful of documented Inuit people to serve in the First World War. He was earmarked for greatness as a sniper and scout. Shiwak's family hailed from a little settlement four miles north of Rigolet, Labrador. The family's original name, Shikoak, meant "thin ice." The family name was changed by an outsider doctor, supposedly for ease of pronunciation.

Training in marksmanship was child's play for Shiwak, said his great-nephew Robert Shiwak. "With his first shot, he put a hole in the middle of the bull's eye. With his second shot, there was still just one hole. They said, 'You missed.' He said, 'I put it in the same hole.'" That marksmanship was honed in the wilds of Labrador. From salmon to caribou, seal, partridge, or rabbit, for the Inuit, hunting was a serious business. You got what you aimed for, Bob Shiwak said.

"Bullets were not plentiful. When they put up the gun, that was food on the table. When you went to get something for the table, that shot counted—they were crack shots," Bob Shiwak said, recalling his own father's determination to always get at least seven or eight ptarmigan with one shot.

"These guys rarely ever missed—ninety-nine per cent of the time they got their target. They were snipers. When he went off to war, they didn't know what to think of him. When he put his gun up to fire it, he might only see a couple inches of a German head, and he'd pick 'em off. His gun was so full of notches, he didn't have room to put another notch," Bob Shiwak said.

In the Battle of Cambrai, on November 21, 1917, John Shiwak and a handful of other soldiers were ambushed on a canal bank at Masnières, France. Shiwak perished along with six other soldiers. Temporary graves at the site were obliterated under intense repeated shelling.

A residential wing at Memorial University of Newfoundland was named Shiwak Hall in his honour in 2014.

John Shiwak's name is one of 820 with no known graves from Newfoundland and Labrador's 1st Battalion on the bronze caribou monument at Beaumont-Hamel Newfoundland Memorial.

Passchendaele

The numbers were horrific at Passchendaele. Over a hundred days in late 1917, almost half a million men died to gain just eight kilometres of brutally contested ground. Four men were killed for every metre of that road. Just the final nine hundred metres took 2,238 casualties. Renamed Canada Avenue, it's less than a kilometre from the farm to the church on the village square. A memorial there is marked by a massive block of Canadian granite—almost as hard as war itself. "And finally in 1917 the Ypres sector came to the climax of its story in that tragedy of blood, mud and futility, the Passchendaele offensive," wrote Charles Henry Savage of Eastman, Quebec, who fought with the 5th Canadian Mounted Rifles in the Second Battle of Passchendaele, between October 26 and November 10, 1917. Four thousand Canadian lads died; another 12,000 were wounded.

No Time for Tenderness

In the confusion of battle, survival at Passchendaele took on a surreal quality for John Pritchard Sudbury of Montreal, Quebec. He had served with the 9th Canadian Brigade Machine Gun Company at Ypres, the Somme, and Vimy Ridge—but Passchendaele was a step down into hell for Sudbury.

"Amid the din of the bursting shells I called to Stephens, but got no response and just assumed he hadn't heard me. He was never seen or heard from again. He had not deserted. He had not been captured. One of those shells that fell behind me had burst and Stephens was no more," Sudbury wrote in a memoir.

"A few paces ahead a shell hole on my right attracted my attention and horror. There was that curly head face downwards on one side of the shell hole, and his body on the other. There was no time for grief or tenderness," he wrote.

In another shell hole were two live Germans, but only just alive, Sudbury said. "They were mere boys and could not have been more than sixteen years of age, both bleeding profusely, but the look in their eyes I have never been able to forget... abject fear mingled somehow with pity. I remember I hastily grabbed my water bottle, drank a sip and threw it to within their reach."

Suddenly, Sudbury felt a bang and toppled into a shell hole. At the same moment, and at his right side, a soldier nicknamed Chips yelled, "Oh, my wrist!" Sudbury realized his left leg was useless, and they had both been hit by the same bullet.

"It was just one stretch of water interspersed with rings of earth here and there, which I knew were the edges of shell holes and I must keep out of them or drown... How I kept my bearings I shall never know... How long that quarter of a mile took me to traverse I do not know," he wrote.

At last, a friendly voice called, "Suds!" Seven soldiers were all that were left of their twenty-seven going in.

"Shells fell all around us and none of us expected to reach the dressing station, only three hundred yards away. It was four hours before we did reach it. The stretcher was full of water, mud and blood; at one halting I managed to slap a field dressing, dragged from the lining of my tunic, on to my knee to try and stop the bleeding. At long last we made it, and to me the very worst kind of hell upon earth was over."

Infected in the mud, Sudbury's gangrenous leg was eventually amputated.

Why Me?

Between September 17 and December 22, 1917, Joseph Boucher of New Brunswick made no journal entries. He was too busy capturing Passchendaele Ridge, where they took prisoners. Air raids on that front were common, Boucher said. "One of the raids made by the Germans on themselves as they dropped most of their bombs in an enclosure where about fifty German prisoners had been put overnight, the intentions being to send them away in the morning. Most of them were either killed or wounded. It was really too bad but no fault of ours," he said.

Once he counted nearly one hundred planes, looping and swooping, dogfighting overhead. "Every once in a while one would come fluttering down like a wounded bird shot in flight," Boucher wrote.

He was wounded twice, mentioned in dispatches, and received the British Military Medal before returning home on storm-tossed seas in February 1919.

"I often wonder why the Lord let me live and so many good men lost their lives," he would later write.

Super Sniper

Neither a wing nor breath stirred in the small hours of No Man's Land, but silent feet traced a path. The war's top sniper was patient and still as a hunting owl in the starless night, waiting long, aiming true. In the Memorial Museum of Passchendaele (MMP17), an oil portrait of Company Sgt. Maj. Francis Pegahmagabow of the Shawanaga First Nation

hangs on the wall. Pegahmagabow was the most successful sniper of the First World War. His gun, one of the much-maligned Ross rifles, stopped a record 378 enemy soldiers. He captured three hundred enemy soldiers. "Peggy" Pegahmagabow overcame discriminatory practices "exempting" Indigenous people from the "eligibility" to enlist, signing up in the first wave of Canadians to volunteer in August 1914. He was one of the first Canadians of the war to be awarded the British Military Medal. His commendation reads: "He carried messages with great bravery and success during the whole of the actions at Ypres, Festubert, and Givenchy. In all his work he has consistently shown a disregard for danger, and his faithfulness to duty is highly commendable." Wounds at the Somme couldn't stop him. At Passchendaele in 1917, he earned his first bar to the Military Medal. He earned a rare second bar to the Military Medal at the Battle of the

Scarpe in August 1918 at Orix Trench, going over the top under heavy
fire to bring back ammunition to assist in repulsing heavy enemy
counterattacks.

After the war, Pegahmagabow served the Wasauksing First Nation
as Chief, leader, and organizer. He was an outspoken advocate for
Indigenous rights and self-determination. A bronze statue at Parry
Sound shows Pegahmagabow with his Ross rifle, a caribou beside him,
an eagle on his arm.

Brave Rush

There's a park named for Private James Peter "Pete" Robertson, Victoria Cross. And a street. And a Canadian Coast Guard patrol vessel.
And a lake. Born in Albion Mines, Nova Scotia, and later a resident of
Medicine Hat, Alberta, he was a CPR railway engineer known for his
wonderful singing voice.

The call went out on November 6, 1917, as they made their way to
the Belgian village of Passchendaele. It was an actual uphill battle. "We
need 27th Battalion volunteers to take out a German gun picking off
Canadian soldiers." Pete was first to raise his hand. His platoon was
held up by uncut wire. Alone, he dashed through an opening on the

flank, rushing the machine gun. After a life-or-death struggle with its crew, he captured the gun then trained it on its former proprietors. His gallantry enabled the platoon to advance, said the *London Gazette* on January 8, 1918. Two of his battalion's snipers were wounded and exposed in German counterattacks. Robertson ventured into danger and brought one back safely. Enemy fighters trained their sights on him then. At great cost to himself, he went back for the second soldier and was hit under heavy fire. He fell. Staggered back up. Lifted the injured sniper to his shoulder and headed back toward the safety of the Canadian line. Slipping and stumbling, he lay the man down to safety. A shell exploded nearby, killing Robertson. "They said he was a humble type of person, that he wouldn't have seen it as bravery—just what needed to be done," said his great-niece Lynne Rockwell Tebay.

Out Past the Onions: Memorial to the Fighting 85th

Wide enough for two to walk, or one to walk and one to pass, a spindly pan-handle hewn of neatly manicured luxuriant lawn amid newly harvested dirt fields of Belgian root vegetables. There, you'll find the Passchendaele memorial to the Nova Scotia Highlanders—the Fighting 85th Canadian Infantry Battalion. In October 1917, some six hundred men earned the nickname Neverfails when they fought to the bloody nub at Passchendaele. While 600 went in, 148 were killed, 280 were wounded, and 85 of the dead have no known grave. Their motto, *Siol na fear fearail*, is Gaelic for "Breed of manly men." A sharp left turn just past the onions leads to a solid stone monument put up by the surviving peers, a tribute to fallen brothers. For the boys who were left, more terror followed, and more valour ensued. *Siol na fear fearail*. Battle Honours for the Neverfails: Arras, Vimy, Ypres 1917, Passchendaele, Scarpe 1918, Amiens, Drocourt-Quéant, Hindenburg Line, Canal du

Nord, Valenciennes, Sambre. Their first battle was capturing Hill 145: in April 1917, they went over where the Vimy Memorial sits now. They are perpetuated by the Cape Breton Highlanders.

Step into History: The Passchendaele Museum

Near modern-day Zonnebeke, Belgium, crosses call to mind grazing sheep flocking the now-pastoral countryside. The gentle landscape is dotted with graveyards. Other than memorials and gravestones scattered over hillocks left by trenches and craters, there are few signs remaining of the chaos of a century ago. Tucked among quiet streets is the restored chateau that has become the Passchendaele Museum. There you may try on a Commonwealth helmet. Feel the weight of it on your head. Hoist unwieldy protective armour (no Kevlar for those warriors). You can sniff harmless versions of lethal gases. Touch and smell the war. You can step down with big steps that are hardly more than a ladder, into restored underground dugouts, into many metres of trenches and carved-out, cave-like tunnels like mine shafts. There are a few mossy signs of life amid the decay on ancient sandbags. It's eerie, walking where war was mined, where another generation lived underground. So many young men clambered into the trenches; fewer clambered out.

Take to the Skies

Kolkata-born Indra Lal "Laddie" Roy was a London schoolboy when war broke out. A gifted student whose design for a better trench mortar received notice and helped earn him an Oxford scholarship, he was keen to fly and sought to join the Royal Flying Corps. He sold

प्रथम विश्व युद्ध में भारतीय भारत INDIA 2019

Indians in First World War

1500

ले. इन्द्रलाल रॉय, डीएफसी

Lt. Indra Lal Roy, DFC

his motorbike to pay for a second opinion on his eyesight after being excluded as unfit to fly. He won his place in the clouds and a post with the RFC's No. 56 Squadron, flying SE5 Scouts, quickly earning victories and a reputation as an "ace." On July 22, 1918, he was shot down over German territory by four enemy Fokker D.VIIs. According to Sanchari Pal, writer at TheBetterIndia.com, the Red Baron (Manfred von Richthofen) paid his respects and sent flowers—a wreath dropped where Roy's plane had crashed. Roy was posthumously given the Distinguished Flying Cross. He is buried at Estevelles, one hundred kilometres north of the grave of another Indian combat pilot of the era, Lt. Shri Krishna Welinkar. Indra Lal Roy's nephew, Subroto Mukerjee, would serve as a fighter pilot in WWII and become the first Chief of Air Staff of the Indian Air Force. Roy was honoured with an Indian stamp on the one-hundredth anniversary of his birth.

July and August in March: Julius Bauer and August Buhler

At Germany's Rancourt Deutscher Soldatenfriedhof, a cemetery for German soldiers, there are two mass graves of 7,492 soldiers. Less than a third of them are known by name. Among the named, Jewish and Christian soldiers are buried side by side. Lieutenant Julius Bauer was one of nine German soldiers with a Jewish gravestone, complete with Hebrew letters, out of 11,422 gravestones. By his side, musketeer August Buhler lies under a Christian gravestone. Both men are named for months—July and August. Good German soldiers, they died as comrades in March 1918.

The two men were not so different, brothers-in-arms at the Second Battle of the Somme, doing what their country asked of them. They were buried side by side—Julius under a Star of David, August under a cross. Two decades later, that difference in religion would be an excuse for war on a global scale.

Seven Pebbles

Seven pebbles, small solid stones, were laid in remembrance atop a Portland stone headstone at Lijssenthoek Cemetery. Stones, not fleeting like breath, but lasting, like memory, enduring, like souls. The stones laid over the Star of David on the headstone of Abraham Slowe of the King's Own Yorkshire Regiment are an example of traditional Jewish gestures of respect. According to jewsfww.com, Slowe "had a great sense of his duty and he carried it out to the last," as written by his commanding officer, W. Scott Hill, in a note to Slowe's mother.

Dogged Optimism: More Lives Than a Cat

A more prime example of dogged optimism could hardly be found than in Ontario soldier Walter Thomas Robus. He had more lives than a cat. He didn't just do his bit: Robus was the first man in town to sign up for the war, joining the "Suicide Club"—the First Canadian Contingent bomb squad—and he apparently took the nickname to heart. Indefatigable, the British-born Robus took blistering punishment in injuries that would sideline the most dedicated soldier—and he kept coming back for more. He saw the Second Battle of Ypres and the Somme and spent a fair amount of time crawling close to the German lines armed with a pistol and pockets full of bombs. His bouts with wounds are confirmed in Robus's government medical records, which also cite episodes of tonsillitis and influenza. There are several mentions in his records that he was "dangerously ill."

In July 1915, he wrote to Reverend A.M. Irwin of Norwood, Ontario:

"I received a bomb in the face. It did not explode but cracked the jaw bone and cut my mouth, and broke my teeth up on one side...

rather painful, still I must not grumble... If I had not have moved as I did I should have got it in the head and would have probably been killed, but it was not to be and so therefore I am spared. After about six weeks I elected to be sent back to the line, and here I am, nearly as fit as ever and ready to do a little more to help crush the Boche."

In February 1916, he wrote that he first thought he would lose his right leg, "but they have fixed it up pretty good; two of the pieces made lovely holes right through the thigh, one about the size of a twenty-five-cent piece and the other bigger, fairly let the daylight into me."

By March 1916, he had had three months of electrical treatment for his legs. "I am trying to get out at the end of the month and rejoin the Battalion in France; I still walk with a limp but can consider myself very lucky to get off with that," he wrote.

Not being one to look for a "blighty" wound that would take him away from the dangers of the Front, he was disappointed when told he was permanently unfit in May 1916. "But I managed to come away with a little persuasion; think I have done my bit already, but something made me come again, don't know why..."

In June 1916, he was injured yet again. "I got a shrapnel bullet clean through shoulder, and my badge saved it from going through my neck, so I am once more on my back for a week or two; still I am doing fine and hope to have another crack at Fritz in the future," he wrote.

In September, he was in hospital, once again marked unfit for further active service. "But when I feel a bit stronger I shall try again for the Front, as I like it better than these hospitals. Enclosed is a small trench snap taken at Messines, showing myself in shirt sleeves; all the others in the picture are killed."

In November 1916, Robus wanted another kick at the can. He had his own peculiar definition of luck. "Asked to be given another trip to France, but they just laughed at me and told me they wanted fit men, so I guess I have to take a back seat. Am trying very hard to get a chance in one of the tanks, may strike it lucky."

In January 1917, he was impatient to get some bars on his chest. "Did you notice one of my bombers [Lou Clarke of Winnipeg] gained the VC and several have DCMs and military medals? So far I have not had the luck, so would like another turn."

In February 1917, he was asked to go to London to do clerical work. "But I have thought the whole matter over seriously, and have decided to carry on for a while till I get a little stronger physically... I think I will take another chance—in fact, something seems to call me back again. I have had that same feeling each and every time I have been back to France, and somehow I think a fellow, when he feels that way, ought to go. Mind you, nobody wants to be shot at, have had quite sufficient, but we old boys took the oath when we enlisted and we have a lot of debts to pay, so those of us that are left must and will finish what our comrades who have fallen cannot do. They have given their all, their life's blood, and we have to fight on," he wrote.

In June 1918, Robus was back at the Front, despite his superiors' misgivings. "I have managed after a struggle to get back again to France and hope to be able to present Fritz with a few souvenirs soon... there is no danger as to the ultimate ending to this show; personally, I feel just as optimistic now as when I first came across, and in fact a little more so."

In 1926, his pastor friend attributed Walter Robus's premature death at age thirty-three to the hardships of his service.

Family Sacrifice: Far from Pleasant

With several brothers and brothers-in-law at the Front, there was an anxiety factor for schoolmaster-turned-officer Charles Henry Savage. "I had many friends and relations in these battalions and it was impossible to pass by a body without a glance at the face to see if by any bad luck it was of one of these. The alternations of fear and relief that this caused were far from pleasant," Henry wrote. "It was much better not to know where one's brothers were. As long as we were on this front I used to worry my head off each time the Germans started shelling the area where I knew he was. I can't imagine anything more nerve-wracking than having a brother in the same unit."

Indeed, for families with more than one child at war, dreaded news sometimes came in twos or threes—or worse.

Family of Service

The Bell-Irving family of British Columbia, founders of the Anglo-British Columbia Packing Company, was all in for the Great War. Their daughter Isabel went to Britain to nurse wounded soldiers. All six brothers enlisted as soon as they could. Henry, Roderick, Malcolm, Duncan, Richard. The youngest, Aeneas, joined when he was old enough. All became officers, all decorated for bravery. Just one, Major Roderick Ogle Bell-Irving, didn't survive the war—he was killed in action and buried at Éterpigny.

Please Send My Brother Home

The *Daily Mail* called James Bell a "real-life Private Ryan." The Bell family—based in Haworth, England—lost four out of five sons before a sister, Annie Bell, wrote a letter to her sole remaining brother's commanding officer, begging for mercy: "My dear sir, I am writing to appeal for your assistance to ask you to send my brother, No. 1186 Driver James Bell, 4th Australian Ammunition Sub. Park AIF, France, back to Australia. He has been in the firing line three years and has a wife and two children in England receiving no separation allowance. He has had three brothers killed. Another has been missing two years last September. He is the only one left out of five brothers. Hoping to solicit your help." The plea was heeded: James Bell was returned to Australia early in 1918 to live a long life.

An Unwilling Sacrifice

The Beechey family of Lincolnshire, England had eight sons, losing five of them to the war. Five crosses were hewn from stone salvaged from the Lincoln Cathedral to be placed where they died around the world. One cross was for Lance Corporal Harold, twenty-six, a farmer and ANZAC (Australian and New Zealand Army Corps) who survived Gallipoli only to die of a whiz-bang on the Western Front. One for Private Charles, thirty-nine, a teacher and naturalist—dead from wounds in the chest at Dar es Salaam, Tanzania. One for 2nd Lieutenant Frank, thirty, a teacher and cricketer. He died doing the tricky job of repairing communications cables between trenches in France. One for Sergeant Barnard, thirty-eight, a mathematician and teacher killed in action at Loos. One for Rifleman Leonard, a railway clerk with the London Irish Rifles. His fatal wounds were sustained in an enemy gas attack near Rouen, France. His last words in a note, according to TheLincolnshireRegiment.org, were, "My darling mother, don't feel like doing much yet. Lots of love, Len."

When thanked by Queen Mary for her sacrifice, their mother, Mrs. Amy Beechey, replied in a few terse words: "It was no sacrifice, ma'am. I did not give them willingly."

Reprieve Too Late

Daniel and Catherine Alty of Westhead, England, were devastated to learn two of their sons had been lost. First, Private Thomas Alty, thirty-two, a gunner with the Tank Corps, was killed in action on November 23, 1917, at Cambrai. Then, their middle son, 2nd Lieutenant Daniel Alty, thirty-one, with the 2nd Battalion South Staffordshire Regiment, died September 5, 1918. He was buried at the Anneux British Cemetery. The Altys applied for home service for their one remaining son, Henry, twenty-four. Their request was granted, even though Henry, winner of the Distinguished Conduct Medal, was loath to leave his fellows in arms. Before he could be pulled back from the Front, Henry was killed in action just weeks before Armistice, on September 30, 1918—the very same day his parents' application for home service was approved.

War and Politics: Conscription, American Style

War and politics have ever been hand-in-glove—with the debate still on as to which is the hand and which the glove. From the vote to go to war to official decisions about how to treat the returning soldiers, politics of the homefront were connected to the Western Front.

In the US, the *Selective Service Act of 1917* was passed by Congress on May 18, 1917. The initial net was for men ages twenty-one to thirty. This was later doubled, going to men from ages eighteen to forty-five. There was a complicated and graduated series of excluders.

Easiest pickings: unmarried with no dependents, or married with self-sufficient wife and no kids under age sixteen. Temporary deferments could be granted men with a dependent wife or child, with sufficient resources to make it without him. Temporarily exempted, but available for service, were local officials, those in agricultural labour or essential war services, and sole providers with dependent parents or dependent children under sixteen. Exempted due to extreme hardship were men married with children or a wife with not enough resources to survive without him, and men with a deceased spouse or deceased parents, making them the sole provider for children or siblings under sixteen. Exempted and ineligible were state or federal officials, licensed working pilots, clergy, ministry students enrolled before May 18, 1917, medically or mentally disabled, "morally unfit," men convicted of treason, felony, or infamous crime.

The American military at this point was entirely segregated, with white supremacist politicians (in the South, particularly) opposed to military roles for Black Americans. They were eventually included in the draft, with more than two million signing up by September 1917. Draft board officials were ordered to tear off a corner of the form to show the draftee was Black and due to be segregated, regardless of qualifications. In the US Marine Corps, Black volunteers were completely excluded, full stop. In the US Navy, Black draftees were assigned menial work only. In the army, most were assigned to labour work, except for two Black combat units—the 92nd and 93rd divisions.

Conscription au Canada

In Canada, the *Military Service Act* in August 1917 brought men between ages twenty and forty-five to the draft pool—and polarized voters for the December 1917 election, which the incumbent prime minister Robert Borden won over Wilfred Laurier (but not in Quebec). The 1917 debate around conscription was divisive along several demographic fault lines in Canada. Immigrants who weren't British, French Canadians, and many working-class workers were typically in opposition. More likely to be in favour: British immigrants, older Canadians, and those aligned with Prime Minister Robert Borden and his Cabinet. Opposition and support were on a spectrum that extended at either end to limits of civility, complete with name-calling.

Eventually, in January 1918, Canada's Indigenous men were exempted from combatant duties, in consideration of former treaties and alliances with the British that promised no forced conscription. Many were already at the Front, however, excelling in their roles.

The *Wartime Elections Act* enabled Canadian women related to soldiers a new opportunity: the vote. The *Military Voters Act* gave military

➤ *Yukon's Martha Black tries a machine gun and scores 64 hits out of 75 at Witley Camp.* YUKON ARCHIVES, GEORGE BLACK FONDS, 81/107 #56

personnel and nurses the vote, regardless of their tenure in Canada. Borden curried favour with farmers, saying their sons would be exempted from the draft, but went back on his word after the December election, sowing roots of contention in the prairies that would flower in due time. In Quebec, bloody riots at Easter in 1918 killed four and injured many more.

It wasn't all for nothing, exactly, but as the war built to its climax in the Last Hundred Days, not even 50,000 more Canadians would be drafted before Armistice, according to the website for the Canadian War Museum in Ottawa.

Province by province, wartime politics had its own effects.

In a letter to his pen pal on February 21, 1916, Hanna, Alberta rancher George Vowel noted his home province's progress in women's suffrage. "So Alberta is giving the ladies a vote. England will come to it yet, too."

Give the Other Vote to the Sister

Meet Roberta MacAdams, the first woman in the British Empire to introduce and pass legislation: *Alberta's Act to Incorporate the Great War Next-of-Kin Association*, which recognized a veteran's organization. For starters, the *Alberta Military Representation Act* of 1917 designated two at-large seats for the Legislative Assembly of Alberta to represent soldiers and nurses from Alberta serving overseas. War correspondent and suffragist Beatrice Nasmyth encouraged Roberta MacAdams to run and manage her campaign in an already crowded field of twenty

men. MacAdams was commissioned a lieutenant in the Canadian Army Medical Corps. As a staff dietitian at Ontario Military Hospital in Orpington, England, she fed recovering soldiers. Her photo in a nurse's wimple tugged at hearts mid-war, and as campaign slogans go, hers was pretty persuasive: "Give one vote to the man of your choice and the other to the sister. She will work not only for your best interests, but for those of your wives, mothers, sweethearts, sisters, and children after the war. Remember those who have helped you so nobly through the fight." MacAdams served in the Alberta Legislature from 1917 to 1921. Her portrait hangs on the walls of the Alberta Legislature.

We Have Stolen Mrs. Black

Among the women of Yukon who went off to Europe to help, the remarkable Martha Black was a tour de force. The American-born wife of Commissioner George Black, the society matron was long known as the First Lady of Yukon. Kathy Jones-Gates of Whitehorse has spent years researching the Chicago local, who was born to wealth, and pregnant with her third child when she climbed the Chilkoot Pass with an expedition financed by her father. When war broke out, she was active in raising funds to support the troops. When her husband sailed with the last of his Yukon contingent, Martha Black insisted on sailing too—the lone female on a ship with 1,500 men. She won the love of the troops, who sang this song daily, Jones-Gates said: "We have stolen Mrs. Black and we will not bring her back, 'till the Germans quit and when the Allies win, 'till we nail the Union Jack to the Kaiser's chimney stack, and we toast the Yukon daughters in Berlin."

In Britain, Martha Black volunteered with the Canadian Red Cross and the YMCA and lectured to raise money for the war effort. She administered the Yukon Comfort Fund, and visited wounded Yukon soldiers in hospitals, bringing them sweets and cigarettes.

After the war, she returned to Yukon, eventually winning an election as Yukon's Member of Parliament. She was the second woman thus elected—and the first American-born.

Damn the Torpedoes

The First World War's torpedoes were no respecters of persons, class, or gender—or of non-combatant status. On June 27, 1918, the hospital ship *Llandovery Castle* of the Canadian Naval Medical Service was returning to Europe after delivering ill Canadian soldiers home. Torpedoed by German submarine U-86, she sank in ten minutes; escaping lifeboats were targeted, too. Of the 258 aboard, 234 perished—including all fourteen nursing sisters. Among those lost to a watery grave were Margaret Marjory Fraser of the Canadian Army Medical Corps, daughter of the lieutenant governor of British Columbia, and Rena Maud McLean, daughter of Senator John McLean of Prince Edward Island.

Promises to Keep

In British Columbia, women got the vote under Premier Harlan Brewster, whose campaign promises went like this: Give women the vote! Bring in Prohibition! Away with political corruption and patronage in civil service! Improve Workman's Comp! Better labour laws! An MLA for Port Alberni, then MLA for Victoria, Brewster rose from a cannery operator to Leader of the Opposition to the Premier's office. There was no class exemption from war—nor from heartbreak for Harlan Brewster, who was in office long enough to keep his first two promises. He died unexpectedly, in office, on March 1, 1918. Far away in France, his son Ray was a gunner, writing home that he felt helpless to comfort his mother and sister and to tend to the details after his dad's untimely death.

Of three of Ray Brewster's letters also in the Canadaletters.ca collection, one is his note to his sister, a Mrs. Townsend, about his shock after the unexpected notification that their father had died suddenly of pneumonia while in office.

"I have tried in every way possible to get a few weeks' leave, but men are scarce now, and it was impossible. I certainly would have liked to get home for a few weeks to help settle things up," he penned.

Ray Brewster was killed instantly on November 1, 1918, when the gun he was operating received a direct hit.

Two Members of Parliament

Two members of parliament, both lieutenant colonels, were distinguished in battle. Both would die in Flanders while sitting in Parliament, their seats in the Canadian House of Parliament vigilantly protected by voters in the mid-war election.

Lieutenant-Colonel George Harold Baker, age thirty-eight, was the MP for Brome, Quebec. He died a hero's death at Mount Sorrel, at Sanctuary Wood on the Ypres Salient, on June 2, 1916. A bronze statue of him was put up in Parliament in his memory.

On the other hand, Lieutenant-Colonel Samuel Simpson Sharpe, aged forty-five, was the MP for Ontario North. Re-elected in absentia while overseas by twice as many votes as his opponent, Sharpe led his battalion into battle at Vimy Ridge, at Hill 70, at Passchendaele. He saw hundreds of his men die—men he had led, men he had recruited.

On May 25, 1918, while being treated for "nervous shock" at the Royal Victoria Hospital in Montreal, Sharpe jumped through a window to his death. "He gave up his life as truly 'on the field of honour' as if he had fallen in action," declared Stewart Lyon in Toronto's *Globe* newspaper on May 27, 1918. According to the Lucy Maud Montgomery page at ConfederationCentre.com, Canada's beloved author of the Anne of Green Gables series lived in Sharpe's riding and was socially acquainted with his wife, Mabel. Clippings show she followed Sharpe's 116th Battalion. Montgomery set *Rilla of Ingleside*, one of the books in her Anne series, in the First World War.

A sad note in Montgomery's journal reads: "We went to Uxbridge this afternoon to see a military funeral. Colonel Sam Sharpe, for whom I voted last December, was buried. He came home from the Front quite recently, insane from shell shock, and jumped from a window in the Royal Victoria in Montreal. Thousands of people attended the funeral."

At the time, Parliament turned a blind eye and remained silent; to this day few know what to say or do about suicide. Samuel Simpson Sharpe's service would be basically ignored in Ottawa for almost a century.

A full century after Sam Sharpe's death, a sculpted plaque of him was installed at Parliament; it was the creation of sculptor Tyler Briley, a former first responder who lives with post-traumatic stress disorder. An annual Sam Sharpe Breakfast in Ottawa now helps MPs learn more about mental wellness issues among service members and veterans. As co-founder of the Sam Sharpe Breakfast with Lieutenant-General The Honourable Roméo Dallaire, Durham, Ontario MP Erin O'Toole said, "Parliament recognizes that service in uniform can lead to both physical and mental wounds. Parliament can send a clear signal of support to people suffering with mental health issues by righting this wrong."

A Close, Close Call

Calls don't get much closer than this: a bullet went through one side of Mahlon Baker's face, fractured both his upper and lower jaw, took out his tongue and teeth, and exited out the other cheek.

On April 13, 1918, he encountered a very young German soldier. "He thought that the boy's age was twelve or thirteen," said Baker's granddaughter, Diane Maidment of Yellowknife, NWT. "They faced each other. My grandfather was shot through the cheek—he lost his tongue and the bullet came out the other cheek," Maidment said.

On Baker's medical record with the Royal Newfoundland Regiment, it was called a "GSW to the face." It was touch and go for Baker, who went from bad to worse before finally turning the corner. He was in the hospital for months. A gunshot wound to his arm, while not the top priority, caused permanent nerve damage that made it difficult to hold a strong grip.

He was twenty-two and considered a hundred per cent disabled.

Somewhere along the way, while he was in the service, his name was changed to Malcolm.

Life was still ahead for the young fisherman. He returned to Newfoundland with his head still in a splint. He owned the first automobile in Elliston, became a taxi driver, married a lovely girl named Naomi, had nine kids, and lived into his eighties.

Diane Maidment recalled her grandfather as a wonderful man not to be held back by disability.

"He struggled a bit, but he always made himself understood," she said.

7

FINAL PUSH
THE LAST ONE HUNDRED DAYS

One Pilgrim's Progress: Escape

Escape from a German prisoner of war camp led to pain and deprivation for Lance Corporal Robert Rollo Paul. He and Private W. Waters of the 2nd Canadian Mounted Rifles Battalion were taken captive at Hooge, near Ypres. After seventeen months in captivity, they made a break, crawling into a nearly impenetrable thicket.

"The words of Bunyan in describing the process of Christian up the Hill of Difficulty and afterwards through the Valley of the Shadow of Death could here be quoted," Paul wrote in his memoir. They kept their eye on the distant northwest. At one point, they were in a swamp so boggy they had to hold hands to avoid being quagmired.

"In the deep darkness, drenched through and through, uncertain of our way, weary to the stage of acute pain, peevish to the extent of abusing one another, chilled in spine and to the point of resolving to give ourselves up to the first authorities, we crawled about for hours, until, just on the verge of complete exhaustion, we suddenly found ourselves in a farming country," Paul wrote.

They ran into a German soldier on leave. He asked for a light for a cigarette. In return, he gave them each a Belga cigarette.

"Early on the eleventh night… knowing that before morning we should be either in the land of freedom or again in the hands of the military authorities of Germany, doomed to days of imprisonment, starvation and cruelty, and, afterwards, to work far more severely than that of the slave at the galleys or in the cottonfields," Paul wrote. In an effort to avoid a German sentry, Paul and Waters went silent, and lost each other in the darkness. Eventually, a kind Dutch woman let Paul in, gave him food and a warm place to rest—and directions to freedom.

Robert Paul made it back to England, as did his running buddy. He later penned a memoir of his captivity and escape.

Keep Your Mouth Shut!

Secrecy alone could ensure the critical element of surprise. This was particularly true as the Allies doubled down on the Germans in what's come to be known as the Last Hundred Days, to be launched August 8, 1918 near Amiens. In July 1918, Army Form W.3066, with the heading KEEP YOUR MOUTH SHUT!, was affixed to paybooks to remind everyone that German spies could be anywhere, disguised as Allied soldiers or placed where they could overhear chatter.

"When you know that your unit is making preparations for an attack, don't talk about them to men in other units or to strangers, and keep your mouth shut, especially in public places," the flyer admonished.

"Do not be inquisitive about what other units are doing; if you hear or see anything, keep it to yourself. If you hear anyone else talking about operations, stop him at once. The success of the operations and the lives of your comrades depend upon your SILENCE."

The admonishment was heeded so well that soldiers separated from their units had a hard time finding them, says Charles Henry Savage in his memoir. "To ask anyone on the road where such and such a battalion was would generally bring the reply, 'Keep your mouth shut,'" he writes.

"The night before the show I was waiting at a crossroads, near our assembly position, for one of our lorries which was bringing up an extra machine gun from the transport lines. There were thousands and thousands of troops in the immediate neighbourhood and I was decidedly surprised when a figure appeared out of the dark and said, 'Are you Captain Montizambert?' As Eric Montizambert was by way of being my future brother-in-law, and as I had never succeeded in running across him in France, this seemed quite a coincidence. I said, 'No, do you expect him here?' But all I got back as the figure disappeared into the dark was 'Keep your mouth shut.'"

Armageddon in the Argonne

Caught by the enemy in the cove of a hill in the Forest of Argonne, October 8, 1918, Sergeant Alvin York did not run. He sank into the bushes, then emerged to single-handedly fight a battalion of German machine gunners. He made them come down that hill to him with their hands in air. There were 132 of them left, and he marched them, as prisoners, into the American line. Marshal Ferdinand Foch, in decorating him, said, "What you did was the greatest thing accomplished by any private soldier of all of the armies of Europe." A corporal at the time, York earned the American Medal of Honour for capturing the German machine gun nest. A biopic with Gary Cooper was a hit years later. The homespun hero looked back on his time at the Argonne: "God would

never be cruel enough to create a cyclone as terrible as that Argonne battle. Only man would ever think of doing an awful thing like that. It looked like 'the abomination of desolation' must look like," York wrote.

"And all through the long night those big guns flashed and growled just like the lightning and the thunder when it storms in the mountains at home. And, oh my, we had to pass the wounded. And some of them were on stretchers going back to the dressing stations, and some of them were lying around, moaning and twitching. And the dead were all along the road. And it was wet and cold. And it all made me think of the Bible and the story of the Antichrist and Armageddon. And I'm telling you, the little log cabin in Wolf Valley in old Tennessee seemed a long, long way off."

His Burden of Leadership

Surrounded by the enemy in the Ormont woods of the Argonne forest, Company B of the US 114th was caught in a ravine on October 12, 1918. The Germans opened fire all around; a slaughterhouse ensued. Captain William Joseph Reddan was ordered to hold the position with his troops near Verdun. The brigade commander insisted; the company counted on help to come from headquarters. The casualties piled high; the support Reddan hoped for failed to come. When the grim smoke cleared, the losses were devastating. Of two hundred men, just thirteen reappeared. Near mad with grief, he vowed to avenge his decimated crew. He had to be restrained; his superiors were concerned for his safety and sanity.

Reddan was awarded the Silver Star for distinguishing himself by gallantry in action.

He made it back home to New Jersey when the war was over, to his children and his wife. In 1936, he wrote *Other Men's Lives: Experiences of a Doughboy 1917–1919*. Memories of those slaughtered soldiers haunted him for the rest of his life.

Envisioning a Future after the War

An elastic-bound notebook recorded the dreams of many a soldier on the front lines. Thoughts of the future were, for many, a happy distraction from hell breaking loose all around. For Signaller Harold Monks Sr., it meant holding onto those thoughts while huddling in a trench.

He notated the signals for Morse code. Those would come in handy after the war with his work as a relief telegraph operator and linesman on the government telegraph at Tofino, BC. Monks' collection is documented at canadianletters.ca and includes jottings pencilled in battlefields at places like Amiens, Scarpe, Canal du Nord, and Canal de Saint-Quentin.

Stephanie Ann Warner researched her grandfather's war experiences. Among the family treasures she found a photo of Monks and buddy Ross McCannel clowning it up. Penned on the back: "No girls here, so we have to make the best of it."

Monks was with the Canadians as the 3rd Brigade, CFA made a final push to capture Valenciennes. In the first week of November 1918, there was intense fighting with heavy casualties. Among the dead, Harold's friends from Vancouver Island: Ray Brewster (November 1) and Ross McCannel (November 6).

"Snapshots in Harold's collection show them joking around at Camp Petawawa in the summer of 1917. Now they were buried in makeshift graves with wooden markers near the battlefield. After the war was over and cameras were allowed on the battlefield, Harold took snapshots of these graves, and carried them in a small leather notebook," Warner told me.

"Harold continued his friendships with both these families after the war, showing that life goes on," she said.

Someone Else's Journal, Someone Else's Souvenirs

Many a soldier brought home some small spoil of war. In the movie *Sgt. Stubby* (2018), one of the American soldiers grabs an Iron Cross medal from the chest of a German prisoner of war and then presents it to

Stubby, saying, "This is yours now." According to historian author Tim Cook in his book, *Victory 1918: The Last 100 Days*, the most popular "souvenirs" were German helmets, Luger pistols, and Iron Cross medals.

Nanaimo, BC, Voluntary Aid Detachment (VAD) nurse Alice Leighton wrote to her soldier husband from London, where she was nursing soldiers blinded in the war. "The [German] helmet came all safe and is such a beauty—the men were all so interested in it and I have promised to photograph most of them with it on," she said.

In his engaging memoir, Charles Henry Savage wrote about missing a man from their fast-travelling run dodging German bullets to get to the safety of a windmill. He spied a shell hole where the man might be hunkering down. "Perhaps he had been wounded and crawled into them, poor fellow... He was in the shell hole alright, and he was the only man whom I kicked in the army, and that wasn't exactly where I kicked him either! I booted him out of the hole and halfway to the windmill before he out-distanced me. He had noticed two dead Germans in these shell holes and had stopped to go through them for souvenirs!"

When the last hundred days of the war started in August 1918, the Germans were still fighting, but the Allies were winning. It was when they had the Boches on the run, out of paper and needing a journal, that George "Black Jack" Vowel liberated a day journal belonging to a Paul Dilschmann of Weissenfels, Germany. It was partly filled with words he couldn't make out, in a language he didn't understand—but after those first few unfinished pages, a clean slate. White pages, grey grid lines, the kind of pocket notebook one could pick up at any stationer's in Rothenburg ob der Tauber. Or find on a body emptied of its stories by a Lewis gun. Many miles from a stationer's store, the journal's former scribe lay on the shell-scarred field. George snapped up the journal and crossed out addresses that didn't pertain to him. He made notations anyone might make on camping at Beauchamp

le Benix on fields littered with the bodies of the German dead. "The boys must have went through them like a whirlwind." From a vantage point of some height where a half-million men engaged in a desperate fight could be observed at once, he watched the Battle of Cambrai and described it as "the grandest sight. Country blazing fire. Both sides seeing just how much ammo they can waste."

Poor Consolation

The questionable wisdom of higher-ups in battle strategizing in the light of equal forces and strange new tools such as artillery, machine guns, airplanes, tanks, submarines, is a frequent theme of Great War literature. In his absorbing war memoir, Charles Henry Savage wrote that observing fighting around Raillencourt, the Marcoing Line, and Cambrai led to the conclusion that staff had "completely forgotten the strategy of Amiens and was reverting to the old methods of the Somme."

"Men were thrown almost in massed formation against positions defended by hundreds of machine guns. The results were bloody in the extreme. Now we know that the Allies were making a desperate and, as it proved, successful attempt at ending the war before winter set in, and that almost nothing counted but time. A perfect explanation, but cold comfort to the pawns in the game," Savage said.

He watched as a battalion marched up the road in fours to take over a position in St. Olle—before St. Olle had been captured. "The forward sections of the battalion were massacred," he wrote.

Savage recalled getting a strong feeling that he would die in a looming attack.

"I must have been suffering from indigestion or some other depressing ailment, for I had a presentiment, amounting to certainty, that I should be killed during this attack. This was the first, and fortunately, the only time that I had such a feeling. I wrote the letters generally considered appropriate for such feelings and sent them to a friend at Battalion Headquarters, to be posted, or not, according to what fate had in store for me during the next twenty-four hours. I had known quite a few who at various times had had such presentiments and I also knew that they were as often wrong as right, but statistics are poor consolation when you feel that way. The average infantryman was sure that he would be killed sometime, but generally he looked upon that sometime as later rather than sooner; not today or tomorrow, but in the indefinite future. After all, he had only carried over into the war the ordinary human being's attitude toward death: something inevitable but not immediate," he wrote.

A Stamp for Billy Bishop

Perhaps one of the most colourful and prominent Canadian soldiers of his day, Ontario pilot and Victoria Cross recipient Billy Bishop was something of a celebrity. For destroying an astounding seventy-two enemy planes (a figure contested by some historians) and for leading in the air and on the ground, he received the Distinguished Flying Cross: "His value as a moral factor to the Royal Air Force cannot be overestimated," his commendation declared. Highly decorated, his honours included the Distinguished Service Order, the Distinguished Service Order Bar, and from France, the Légion d'honneur and the Croix de Guerre with palm. "His consistent dash and great fearlessness have set a magnificent example to the pilots of his squadron... on all occasions displaying a fighting spirit and determination to get to close quarter with his opponents," his commendations noted. What is often overlooked about Billy Bishop is that as a schoolboy he was known for fighting. He was not a great student. He was considered "easily discouraged." Still, a classic underachiever as a youth, he became a grown-up poster child for persistence and went on to great success both during and after the war. There's a lake named for William Avery Bishop in the Northwest Territories. A park in Ottawa. A mountain in Alberta. A Royal Canadian Legion branch in Vancouver. A hazardous materials training centre at CFB Borden. A hangar in Brampton, Ontario. An entrance at a Hamilton school. A trophy with the Air

Force Association. A squadron of the Royal Canadian Air Cadets in Owen Sound. A building at the 1st Canadian Air Division. A Canadian NORAD Region HQ in Winnipeg, and an airport in Toronto. On top of all that, a smash play and TV show. And perhaps the ultimate compliment: a Canada Post stamp.

Piling on the Years

As a lad, Thomas Ricketts was a fisherman who had quietly added three years to his age to enlist with the Royal Newfoundland Regiment. On October 14, 1918, Private Ricketts volunteered to brave heavy battery fire to advance with the Lewis gun and his section commander. They ran out of ammunition under heavy fire; Private Ricketts's "presence of mind in anticipating the enemy intention and his utter disregard of personal safety" (not to mention his willingness to dash through heavy machine gun fire to fetch more ammo) saved the day. If Private Ricketts—who hailed from Middle Arm, White Bay—had not said he was eighteen when he was fifteen, he never would have been admitted to the RNR. He'd never have been wounded at Cambrai. He would never have become the youngest combat recipient of the Victoria Cross for Conspicuous Bravery and Devotion to Duty or the Croix de Guerre with gold star.

After returning home, Ricketts went to school to become a pharmacist at the corner of Job and Water Streets in St. John's. The pharmacy is gone but the memorial remains to Private Ricketts and his conspicuous bravery and devotion to duty. A century later, a public event at the Thomas Ricketts Memorial at Sint-Eloois-Winkel in Belgium recognized his bravery.

Angel of the Trenches

At two, Joao (John) Baptista DeValles immigrated with his family from the Azores to America. A brilliant student, fluent in six languages, he found his place in the Catholic priesthood, as pastor and parochial school founder in Massachusetts. He enlisted as a US Army Chaplain with the 104th Regiment of the 26th Infantry "Yankee Division." A soft touch, he made "loans" to soldiers, documenting the debts in his journal, then ripping out the notes—eventually earning the nickname "Angel of the Trenches."

In 1918, he put himself repeatedly in harm's way at Apremont, braving heavy artillery and machine gun fire to bring the wounded to safety. When his hands were too numb to carry stretchers, he was known to loop telephone wire to his wrists to hold the stretcher handles. At Chemin des Dames, he rendered gallant service, staying with the wounded during heavy bombardment. One night they found DeValles wounded at the side of a dead soldier to whom he had ministered.

DeValles was given the French Croix de Guerre for "extraordinary heroism and exceptional devotion to duty, under uninterrupted fire and the constant risk of his life," and the French Legion of Honour.

He had no time to rest on his laurels: Father DeValles died in 1920 from complications of wounds in battle and mustard gas. They pinned the US Army's Distinguished Service Cross on his chest in the casket. According to the *Catholic Stand*, all of New Bedford mourned the loss.

Tres Meses Muy Largos

Bernardo Bazan Elizondo lived in rural Starr County, Texas, where his family had lived near Rio Grande City on the Mexican border for many generations. There were many Elizondos there, and Bernardo never received his draft notice, said his granddaughter, Mary Ann Flores. "They came looking for him… They came and handcuffed him and took him; they thought he was trying to dodge the draft."

Elizondo was fighting in the Meuse-Argonne when he was wounded and taken prisoner. "The Americans were cannon fodder… they would go in the open and the Germans would mow them down, and that's what happened to him," Flores said.

He was taken prisoner by the Germans in France on October 5, 1918. Despite Armistice stilling the nations' guns on November 11, 1918, the release of all the prisoners of war took months after Armistice. Elizondo, who was of Mexican American heritage, described his "tres meses muy largos" (three very long months) in a letter home.

Mary Ann Flores recalled that Elizondo returned home to Texas and raised a family in Kenedy, Texas, but his wounds never completely healed. He returned to Sam Houston Army Hospital to have a rib removed, and succumbed to pneumonia in 1933, leaving behind a widow with six young children.

Two thin silver disks—his "dog tags" identifying him as number 3065105—and a leather journal memorialize this Mexican American soldier's three very long months.

8

THE ANIMALS' WAR

Good Horse, Poppy

Articulated metal ribs on the War Horse Memorial, designed by British sculptor Susan Leyland, reflect the deprivations of war. The horse, Poppy, grazes forever at Ascot. She has no fear of flying shrapnel. The memory of the high, ominous whistle of shells is persistent but distant, a haunting echo in her tall bronze ears. There are no more 3,000-pound guns to pull, nor charges to carry her master into. Her eternal hope now is to fatten up on good grass; Poppy has earned green pastures, still waters, carrots. Both indispensable and disposable, eight million horses and mules would die in the Great War—almost one horse per man down. If you asked Poppy, she might question if there was anything "great" about it.

Ballarat

A bronze memorial at Ballarat, Australia honours horses and mules killed in the First World War—and poet Adam Lindsay Gordon. Designed by Raymond B. Ewery, its base is engraved with Job 39:21–22: "He paweth in the valley, and rejoiceth in his strength; he goeth forth to meet the armed men. He mocketh at fear, and is not afraid, Neither turneth he back from the sword." The memorial was erected to mark the one-hundredth anniversary of the poet's living in Ballarat, and as a memorial to the horses and mules killed in the First World War, "including 196,000 that left these shores never to return." According to the Australian War Memorial website, one horse made it back to the land down under—Sandy, the horse belonging to Major General Sir William Bridges (who was killed at Gallipoli.) Sandy was sent from Gallipoli to Egypt to France and then to England, before being sent to live out his days at the Central Remount Depot at Mari-byrnong, Australia. In Canada, a horse named Morning Glory outlived her master, Lieutenant-Colonel George Harold Baker, Member of Par-liament, by catching the eye of top brass. Safe for the war's duration, she returned to graze in Brome, Quebec, after the hostilities ceased.

Early in the war, before the US officially declared war, hundreds of thousands of horses were bought in America by the British and shipped to the Western Front from Newport News, Virginia, the *Daily Press* reported. Like soldiers, horses that died during the sea journey to deployment were buried at sea. "Of the 750 horses taken on board at St. John, seven of them were lost at sea through sickness. Sharks followed us daily after the first horse had been thrown overboard," recorded Joseph Richard Boucher of Kent County, New Brunswick.

A Bond with Their Horses

In the middle of the trench-bound misery, George Vowel would have given something fine to be back in the Bullpound Country, watching his brothers bust broncs at the rodeo. He recounted a litany of horse memories to his pen pal, Bebe: "Not a beauty, Maverick is just a cayuse [a feral or "low-quality" breed] but he is the most intelligent bronco that I ever saw... Not much to look at but he'd do whatever I asked of him," he wrote of the pony that carried his little brothers and sister three astride to the country Red Rose school house. Maverick would

wait outside at the hitching post, patient for his bit of water and hay and the return trip over the dusty prairie road to a modest dugout barn with a sod roof. Like others, George grieved the sacrifice of millions of horses and mules fallen in the spoils of war. The French government came to the Canadian prairies to buy horses for $135 apiece, and

George's father had contributed dozens from the family ranch. According to *The Horse in War and Famous Canadian War Horses* by David Sobey Tamblyn, just 24,000 Canadian mounts survived past Armistice to Belgian government auction. At least 110 officers would bring their chargers home to Canada.

POV: War Horse

The book *War Horse* by British author Michael Morpurgo was a smash hit, written from the perspective of a horse at war. Interviewed on BBC by Fi Glover, Morpurgo said he was inspired in part by Great War veterans he met at a local pub, in part by a haunting painting by F.W. Reed in 1917 of war horses charging into barbed wire, and in part by a schoolboy whose difficult stammer was overcome by a connection with a horse who seemed to understand the importance of listening to the lad. The idea that the horse might not understand each word but knew the importance of being a listener in the relationship sparked the idea for Morpurgo. His ensuing classic was adapted into an acclaimed Steven Spielberg movie.

The Mystery of the Chestnut Gentleman

Susan Raby-Dunne of Canadian War History Tours is the author of several books about the First World War that are interconnected to Lieutenant-Colonel John McCrae, the Canadian doctor who wrote the most famous war poem, "In Flanders Fields."

One of those books is *Bonfire: The Chestnut Gentleman* (the nickname McCrae gave to his horse). The book follows Bonfire, from his loan by a family that had a stable of fine hunter-jumpers, to the mystery of what happened to him after McCrae died.

Raby-Dunne has a theory based on a little book by Sir Andrew MacPhail, a friend of McCrae's who edited and published some of his work. In his *Essay in Character*, McPhail says Bonfire was honourably and safely retired in a place that the brass need never know about. "It's my belief McCrae's friend Edward Morrison and other influential figures paid some French farmer to retire him," Raby-Dunne says, noting the still-young Bonfire would have been destined for the remount depot, to serve other officers. "I believe the people who would have known what happened to Bonfire—Morrison and MacPhail—never said a word, as it would have been illegal to spirit him away."

Full of Life, Never Gets Tired

On November 22, 1914, while at training on the Salisbury Plain, England (near Stonehenge) James Wells Ross wrote: "Today we had no church parade owing to the cold weather, so we took everyone out for a ride, and it did the horses good ... The horses stand the weather well, but need lots of care and exercise often to keep them warm. I have a fine one now. 'Ben' I call him. He is dark bay, almost black with a star and left ear split for about half an inch. He is full of life and never gets tired."

Despite any hardening effect from war's brutalities, soldiers like James Wells Ross were troubled by the thought of horses dying in a war in which they sought only to serve their masters—and of the fathers and sons and sweethearts of those who met similar fates.

Hitched to a Wagon

A family history compiled by Lloyd G. Ferrel tells of Carl Reuben Showalter of Longville, Minnesota, who served four years—most of the First World War—coming home with a close-call towel that had been in his backpack. It had a bullet hole in it. "He saw a lot of action, and seldom would talk about it, but his job involved driving a team of horses near the front lines. He mentioned once that he had used over a hundred horses, and that eighty of them had been killed while hitched to a wagon," Ferrel wrote.

Canine Heroes: Red Cross Dogs

Furry enlisters, Red Cross dogs were picked for their loyalty and smarts; they had to be keen of nose, and sharp in vision. Thousands trained to ignore heavy fire, to venture despite terror out into No Man's Land, to wear a gas mask, to distinguish between the living and the dead, to recognize a Commonwealth uniform. They could bring medicine and water, and even return with evidence and summon help if an injured man was unable to move. One of the most famous was

an Airedale terrier named Jack who, despite his own mortal wounds, delivered a critical message to save a unit.

Gentleman in Fur

On the cover of the September 1918 *Ladies' Home Journal*, a painting by Carton Moorpark depicts Filax, Red Cross Dog of Honor. Trained to steal out into danger and sniff out the wounded, he would return with an item to find help—and then direct the help to the injured man. The German shepherd was twice wounded at the Western Front, but survived his master. "Could the *Ladies' Home Journal* do less than honor, on its cover this month, Filax, Gentleman in Fur, whose achievements have made him worthy to receive the coveted Croix de Guerre?" the editor asked. "Filax heroically served the American Red Cross on the Western Front for over a year, beloved of his French captain master and of all his upright walking companions." Sadly, after finding a home in New York and a return to domestic tranquility, Filax perished in a kennel fire.

Good Little Fundraiser

Then there was Muggins, a Spitz who raised about $21,000 (almost a quarter million in today's currency) for the war effort at Belleville and Government streets in Victoria, British Columbia.

The Canadian Red Cross mascot would strut proudly around the Inner Harbour with donation boxes tied to his back. According to redcross.ca, Muggins was a popular ferry visitor and had his picture made with the Prince of Wales and Canadian general Sir Arthur Currie. Posed on a fundraising table, a sign beside him read: HELP THE BOYS WHO FOUGHT FOR YOU... I AM NOT CHAINED TO MY JOB, I AM JUST DOING MY BIT. HAVE YOU DONE YOURS?

His silver medal from the Canadian Red Cross Society is engraved on the back: PRESENTED TO MUGGINS FOR FAITHFUL SERVICES RENDERED DURING THE GREAT WAR. Even after his death from pneumonia in 1920, Muggins wasn't done. He was stuffed and mounted, put on display with his medals at the BC Legislature, and his body brought back for active service to raise money for the Second World War.

The Stuff of Movies: Sergeant Stubby

Sergeant Stubby was a regimental mascot for the US 102nd Infantry division—a stray Boston terrier adopted by his American master, Yale student Robert Conroy. He went to war with his master; with his sensitive hearing, he was first to hear the whine of incoming artillery.

Wounded by a grenade at Chemin des Dames, he was given first aid, and sent to the rear to convalesce and brighten morale. He caught rats. After being gassed he was given his own mask, and he learned to detect gas. His legend grew when he caught an enemy soldier by the seat of his pants.

The grateful women of Château-Thierry sewed a little chamois coat for his medals as he was promoted up through the ranks. After the war he went to Georgetown Law with his master, where he was something of a cause célèbre. In his lifetime, Stubby met three American presidents. Stuffed, he lives on a century later at the Smithsonian Museum.

A 2018 computer-animated feature film centres on his life. Directed and co-written by Richard Lanni, *Sgt. Stubby* follows him from life as a stray to adoption and finally, fame and honour as a mascot who even knew how to salute.

From War-Torn Europe to Hollywood

British Author Lucy London commemorates fascinating and often long-forgotten people involved in the conflict at femalewarpoets .blogspot.com. Her exhibit on female poets for a 2012 exhibition at the Wilfred Owen Story museum in Birkenhead, Wirral, England, led to books, blogs, and Facebook pages filled with fascinating facts and heart-touching stories, like the discovery of canine film star Rin Tin Tin by American doughboy Lee Duncan in Alsace. Duncan trained the clever pup and found him work in dozens of silent films, where he was a box-office hit. He also popularized the German Shepherd breed as pets.

Famous Inspiration

Sometimes mascots had an exotic touch. For the 2nd Canadian Infantry Brigade, there was Winnipeg—Winnie, for short. She was an orphaned *Ursus americanus* cub, far from her beloved Canadian woods in White River, Ontario. "It was a time of close calls, thrilling triumphs, painful sacrifice, and great friendship. By war's end, millions knew her name," reads the back cover of *Winnie's Great War: A Novel Based on the True Story of the World's Most Famous Bear* by Lindsay Mattick and Josh Greenhut, with art by Sophie Blackall. Lieutenant Harry Colebourn's fuzzy buddy went on to live to twenty years at the London Zoo. Her most famous friends? None other than A.A. Milne and his son Christopher Robin. Hence, the name for Winnie the Pooh, a most beloved childhood character around the world.

One Tough Pigeon

Automotive inventions changed warfare in obvious ways; while horse and mule power was still used for hauling everything from big guns to food supplies at the Front, truck and tank capabilities made mobilization convenient in new ways. Take the inventive motorized portable dovecote, basically a motorhome for carrier pigeons.

Cher Ami (French for "dear friend") was one of six hundred pigeons trained for the US Army Signal Corps in France. When Charles Whittlesey and the Lost Battalion, the 77th Infantry Division, became trapped in a wooded pocket in the Argonne, behind enemy lines without food or ammunition, dwindling and sure to perish, pigeons bearing the messages "Many wounded. We cannot evacuate," and "Men are suffering. Can support be sent?" were sent out—and shot down. One last pigeon, the famed Cher Ami, a bird of great valour, was given the desperate message to carry: "Our artillery is dropping a barrage directly on us. For heaven's sake, stop! Whittlesey, Maj. 308th." Cher Ami was wounded by shrapnel, shot through the breast, blinded in one eye, but she survived to wing forty-five kilometres to the rear in just twenty-six minutes. The critical delivery saved the 194 surviving men.

Medics scrambled to save her. The French honoured her with the Croix de Guerre with palm and oak leaf cluster. When she left France for well-deserved rest, US general John J. Pershing saw her off. Upon her 1919 death from wounds suffered in battle, the lauded Cher Ami was stuffed; her final loft, the Smithsonian museum. She has her own books, and she is depicted as a character in the 2001 movie *The Lost*

Battalion, directed by Russell Mulcahy, written by James Carabatsos, and starring Rick Schroder. Cher Ami was inducted into the Racing Pigeon Hall of Fame in 1931 and honoured with a gold medal from the Organized Bodies of American Racing Pigeon Fanciers. Her handler in the signal corps, Enoch Clifford Swain, was honoured for his work. In November 1919, she was in a small covey of eight animals (some living, some dead) to be honoured on Capitol Hill by Angels Without Wings and the National Marine Corps League with the Animals in War & Peace Medal of Bravery, a congressional medal created by author Robin Hutton for outstanding American animals in both war and peace.

9

THE END AND WHAT CAME NEXT

Minutes before Armistice

By refusing to declare a ceasefire or truce before Armistice, French marshal and commander in chief Ferdinand Foch left the pressure on—and the death toll continued to rise. Another 11,000 belligerents were wounded or killed in the moments before the world could heave a sigh of relief. The last Canadian killed was Private George Price, age twenty-five, from Port William, Nova Scotia, shot by a sniper minutes before Armistice.

The Last Belligerent

The very last man to throw the first punch, the last to go "over the top," was Maryland soldier Henry Gunther, officially the last belligerent in the First World War. Gunther was drafted to the 313th Infantry, Baltimore's Own. His frank description of Front life upon arriving in France in July 1918 had cost him dearly. In a letter, he urged a hometown pal to avoid enlistment. Intercepted by censors at a time when enlistment was still a top priority, the advice earned him a demotion from sergeant to private—and a shame he couldn't shake.

The clock's second hand ticked down on November 11, 1918. The long-hoped-for peace was seconds away. While others were praying or preparing to cheer, getting ready to lay down their arms, Gunther barreled out from under cover at Chaumont-devant-Damvillers in Meuse—bayonet blazing, against orders, headed for the German machine guns, with one minute on the clock in its countdown to Armistice. His friends tried to call him back. Even the German soldiers awaiting the truce, who had him in their sights, tried to wave him off before gunning him down.

Baltimore Sun writer James M. Cain tried to puzzle it out: What had Henry Gunther been thinking? He interviewed Gunther's sorrowful friends. Friends speculated that the shame of the demotion affected him badly. Gunther brooded over his reduction in rank. He was obsessed with making good.

Perhaps, in a way, he did. The Army restored his rank of sergeant and posthumously awarded him a Divisional Citation for Gallantry in Action and the Distinguished Service Cross.

Henry Gunther's remains were reinterred in 1923 at Most Holy Redeemer Cemetery—at home in Baltimore at last.

Bookending the Beginning and the End

An immigrant from England to Toronto, George Walter Adams journaled about the war's beginnings on November 16, 1914: "All city regiments notified to be at armouries at 2:30 this afternoon. As soon as notified, the men had to rush home from their employment, don their uniforms, and hustle to the armouries. The sight of men lacing their boots and putting on their uniforms on the streetcars caused much alarm among the general public, and rumour had it that the Germans were on their way from Detroit to invade Canada."

Adams enlisted as a clerk in October 1916 in Toronto. He was still overseas when his mother, Emily Adams, wrote to tell him what Armistice Day was like back home—on November 11, 1918, at 4:30 AM Toronto time:

"Edie came into my room and said, 'Can't you hear the racket? The Armistice is signed.'... a few minutes after, Nellie, Eva, Zeta, Annie, and Dorothy came with saucepan lids and old tin cans. They made a dreadful noise… went parading the streets till breakfast time… Mr. Wykes sent in to say he was going to burn the Kaiser, would we like to join in the fun. So we all went out, and there was a huge bonfire in front of their house, and when that died down a bit Mr. McCaw brought out a lot of boxes which made it scorching hot."

Pandemic in the Peace

Take an invisible, rapidly spreading virus. Pull together hundreds of thousands of people in close quarters, then disperse them abroad in crowded transport. Send them into street celebrations around the world, without regard for social distancing. That recipe may sound like a twenty-first century pandemic, but it's hindsight, not 2020.

In 1918, a virulent strain of influenza was first observed at Camp Funston in Fort Riley, Kansas, on March 11. Individual cases rapidly boiled over from ordinary flu symptoms into the most shocking pneumonia doctors had seen. The mortality rate was twenty times that of the typical influenza.

All too successfully dispersed worldwide via shipping routes, it was dubbed the "Spanish Flu" because only the Spanish press was allowed to report on the havoc wrought among the general population.

This was a genuine pandemic, easily spread with the help of troops and modern transport. By the time the third wave had washed over the

globe, a fifth of the world was infected. It struck seniors and babies—
and young men in their prime—with particular vengeance, dropping
as many troops as the war itself.

In France, the battle against the flu raged even as opposing sides
prepared for the climactic end that was coming.

In a letter to someone named Angereau, Gavin Gibson Baird
recalled a sickly summer:

"You have no doubt seen from the papers about the MacAlpine
party having been lost on the shores of the Arctic Ocean. I had met
Colonel MacAlpine, the man in charge of this expedition, through
my brother Jack, in London, and the second time I met him was in
France, while I was in hospital. I was awakened the second or third

night while there by the orderlies carrying in a man on a stretcher, and he was groaning so terribly that I felt sure that he would have 'gone west,' as we used to say, by morning. The nurse who was looking after me was a girl from Eastern Canada, and when she came around in the morning I asked her if the man they had brought in during the night had died. She started to laugh and said that he wasn't any worse than I was with the flu. This was the man who was in charge of the Dominion Explorers' machines in the north, and who was lost for practically two months, but was eventually found," he penned.

From Les Fermont in Arras, a Canadian soldier named Cecil Tyrell wrote to his wife on June 29, 1918:

"Budsie Dear: Well, you will notice that I too have missed a week in writing, but my excuse is good, and an honest one. Our ambulance base covered more miles in the last two weeks than they have since we have been in France. We have had three or four moves in the last two weeks, but apart from that, we have been running day and night, hauling Spanish Flu patients. I guess you have read in the papers about the influenza plague. Well, we are certainly getting our share of it in France now… I think Fritz's army is also suffering from the plague from the reports of the prisoners taken lately. In fact, it is rumoured that that was the reason their offensive was given up … We have been sleeping in our cars for a long time, but we don't like to take chances now that we are hauling so many flu patients. I think that is how Harry caught it."

In America, the Red Cross created a national committee to deal with the flu, and they rallied resources from military and civilian sectors.

Public health authorities had just one ace in the hole: People were already accustomed to the demands of nationalism and privations of war—rationing their sugar, sending their sons to fields of slaughter. Foregoing church attendance, working staggered shifts, abbreviating funerals, wearing masks—these were demands they wearily decided they could live with.

On October 22, 1918, Emily Adams of Toronto wrote to her soldier son, George Walter Adams:

"I expect you have heard we have two epidemics—one Spanish Influenza, the other pneumonia. It has become so serious that the-atres and picture shows are closed and churches are only allowed to have one service. The Arlington Hotel is turned into an hospital, also Mossop House. You will be sorry to hear Frank Bresetor died of pneu-monia last week and last Tuesday Harry Tucker died of it at Ottawa. You knew he got exemption until the Parliament Buildings were fin-ished. It seems the previous Saturday Aunt Eva got word that he had the flu, so she and Mabel went to see him. When they got there he had been taken to May Court Emergency Hospital as he had pneu-monia. Fred Hall went to fetch the body and told Charlie there were sixty bodies on the train. Well, Harry was buried last Friday at Mount

Pleasant [cemetery]. Edie and Nora wouldn't let me go to the funeral in case of infection… It certainly is good of Mabel to write you such long letters. Am sorry to say she is still in bed with the flu. Edie phoned Nellie yesterday. She was going on alright but Mrs. Swann is still ill too. Your loving mother, Emily Adams."

Oddly, perhaps the worst setback in the battle against the flu came with Armistice. Wild with joy, people went crazy with the news that on November 11, hostilities had ceased. The flu was forgotten, and so was social distancing. People hugged and kissed neighbours and total strangers alike, and the virus leaped from carrier to victim, hand to shoulder, mouth to cheek.

Guelph, Ontario, soldier Robert Shortreed wrote to his mother the day after Armistice amid Paris throngs:

"You will have heard the good news that the Armistice has been signed, which is at least the beginning of the end if not the end. Anyway, it is being celebrated as the end here. Yesterday Paris was crazy with joy and streets were impassable for people. Today is going to be almost as bad. Flags are to be seen everywhere. The French way of showing their joy is to kiss everyone and few people escaped it yesterday. Of course the soldiers came in for their share. Parades were innumerable, and I was in one of British soldiers headed by the Horse Guards Band, but it was impossible to get through the crowd, and the band did not have a chance to walk let alone play. It was simply a mob all day long," he wrote.

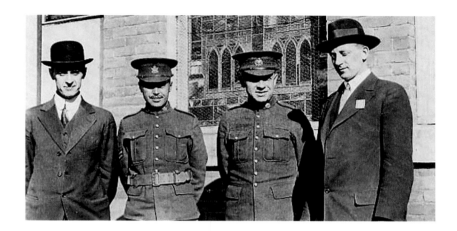

Alice Leighton of Nanaimo, British Columbia, and followed her husband to war. Arthur Leighton, a lawyer, went to the Front, and Alice worked with the VAD to nurse injured soldiers in England. She wrote to him from a London that was crowded to bursting with excitement and activity just after the war ended:

"I have just finished your Peace letter of the 11th. Like you, I can hardly believe it is true... It seems too marvellous that it is all over at last and that I shall have my darling at home with me again... I have just come home from the Coliseum. I took five of the men, and when we got out in the street to come home, there was such a jam I didn't know how I should even navigate them along. Buses were out of the question, and so we decided to try the Tube... We came out at Charing Cross... so jammed I was almost in despair when I saw a taxi unloading just beside me. I rushed up and told the taxi man I had five blind soldiers and must get home."

To Alice, it seemed almost too good to be possible, that the war could be over and her husband could still be in one piece.

"The last week, dearie, has been the hardest I have had for I was so afraid something might happen at the very last. I went down on my knees, dearie, when I knew for sure you were coming back to me."

They returned to Nanaimo after the war—all in one piece.

Finishing Wonderful

In a post-war note, Walter T. Robus was hoping the German Kaiser would get some of his own.

"The peace celebrations here have been immense, everybody frantic with joy and excitement; what a relief to the parents of the boys serving! And what a relief to know the slaughter and suffering are over; Willie [Kaiser Wilhelm of Germany] should be treated as he deserves and not allowed to get away light; the soldiers should have the handling of him... The Canadians finished wonderful," he wrote to the Reverend A.M. Irwin back home in Ontario.

When Robus died young in 1926, his employer put up a bronze memorial plaque in honour of his war service.

See You at the Reunion

Robert Shortreed of Guelph, Ontario was a salesman who enlisted with the 64th Depot Battalion of the Canadian Field Artillery.

During Canada's Hundred Days, Shortreed's 2nd Canadian Siege Battery was snapped in action at Canal du Nord, France on September 27, 1918. In 1975, a group photo at a reunion of the 2nd Canadian Siege Battery in Charlottetown, captures the years. The lines. The glasses. The silver hair. The cane. And the enduring brotherhood of any who suffer a thing together. The generation-jumping photos from the Robert Shortreed collection articulate much about the war without using a word, chronicling a most hideous war in a most unusual past century and the technology that helped rocket us into this one.

Noble Duty Bravely Done: CLC

Records show Wang Hui Lan signed up with the Chinese Labour Corps from Shandong province, and for a few francs a week he helped win the war. Some CLC workers met grim ends clearing land mines; others were fired on while cutting barbwire or slinging bridges. It was probably influenza that brought Wang Hui Lan to hospital months after Armistice, in Lijssenthoek. Or perhaps he was ill from the muddy, distasteful work of digging up Commonwealth bodies from graves that had been torn up by shells, in order to re-inter them in military plots since the war was over.

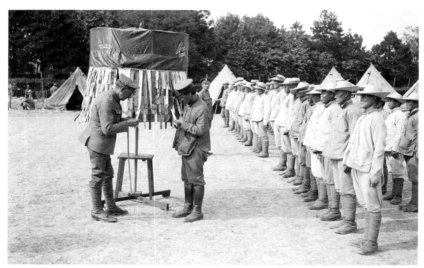

Wang Hui Lan's gravestone suggests more questions than answers. Engraved on Portland stone, his tablet reads: THOUGH DEAD HE STILL LIVETH. This was one of four standard phrases set aside for engraving on the Portland stone of CLC graves. The others: FAITHFUL UNTO DEATH, A GOOD REPUTATION ENDURES FOREVER, and A NOBLE DUTY BRAVELY DONE. There was no anglicized name here, but

Chinese figures and No. 67569 identify him. Commonwealth records show his name was Wang Hui Lan and that he died on April 6, 1919. According to Lijssenthoek.be, the Chinese figures on his headstone translate to "gentle gracious orchid, bloomed too brief, we honour you."

Some 140,000 Chinese men worked for the Allied forces on the Western Front in the First World War in conditions more primitive than those faced by western soldiers. One in seven died. Several thousand stayed in Paris after the war. Most of the rest were repatriated. Five CLC workers were awarded Meritorious Service Medals, including First Class Ganger Liu Dien Chen, who rallied his men under shellfire in 1918. Zhu Guisheng, who died in 2002 at age 106, also served in the French Army during the Second World War.

Coming Home "After They've Seen Paree"

After the initial relief of Armistice, the Allies had another bit of business: the occupation of Germany, particularly prior to the final crossing of the T's in the Treaty of Versailles in June 1919. For some of the soldiers, the sheer absence of the terror of war was a sort of bliss. Oklahoma-born George Vowel wrote in his letters that the land around Europe's tallest cathedral in Cologne was "mighty pretty country."

Post-war Cologne was like being on leave, as far as George was concerned. On New Year's Day in 1919, he noted, "We have been having a great time hunting nearly every day and playing poker nights and a trip into Cologne occasionally."

Others, exhausted from four years of war, were angry and frustrated by the slow pace of repatriation, says author and historian Tim Cook in *Victory 1918: The Last 100 Days*. "Riots and disturbances broke out in the months following the Armistice. These incidents frightened the British authorities into fast-tracking the Canadians' departure."

Worries, set to music, about how veterans would be kept down on the farm after they'd seen Paris could as well have been directed toward Great Britain's class-rigid society.

Once mobilized to fill jobs vacated by soldiers, women who built bombs for the war effort and nursed wounded soldiers around the clock and piloted ambulances around the Front in France were often displaced. Like other demographic groups struggling for civil rights and equality, after a brief shining moment of near-equality during the urgent moment of war, women around the Empire (and beyond) often found it difficult to revert to their pre-war roles, according to the Newfoundland and Labrador Heritage website: "They were often frustrated because their families and communities expected them to return to their domestic roles, but the war had given them a new-found sense of independence and self-reliance. Many joined the suffrage movement, which won Newfoundland women the right to vote in April 1925."

O Little Town of Arkholme

Historian Arthur Mee noted a rarity and named Arkholme in the United Kingdom a "Thankful Village." This village sent fifty-nine of her best sons, fathers, brothers, and sweethearts to face the war monster, and every last man—all fifty-nine—returned home safe, but not necessarily unchanged. The boys they once used to be wanted their years back, but every one slipped past the Grim Reaper and in through the city gates, escaping for the moment the law of an eye for an eye.

Such happy consequence, bucking probabilities. All who went came back. In Arkholme—as any town that had folks at the Front—mothers and fathers and sweethearts had held their collective breaths. Did they pray? Drum fingers? Perhaps they cultivated ulcers and twitches, paced blackout-darkened streets. Bookmakers might pause at the odds for a handful of towns with this phenomenon. A cynic might say "Buy a lottery ticket!" and privately wonder about rates and dates of volunteerism versus conscription. There was no need for survivor's guilt, considering all everyone was subjected to, including all those whose grandfathers returned home but not unscathed. They were different for all they had seen, and each family who had one veteran at a time coming home to brighten their family's doorways made for a Thankful Village.

Tears were due for those whose losses were more bitter, but the homeland rejoiced with those whose blissful statistical anomaly shaped their town's DNA. (Perhaps they wondered if the communal lucky streak would continue—and if it was something in the water.)

The Aftermath of War for Some

After the pounding of shells—after seeing those doing their bit getting blown to bits—after working fruitlessly to secure world peace, only to discover they secured nothing, soldiers came back from the Front scarred in more ways than one. Some found they'd become a little too used to Service Rum Diluted; others discovered absence and abstinence and sexual health don't always go together. The song wondered how they would be kept down on the farm after they'd seen Paris, but having their eyes opened to the wonders of Europe was not the biggest problem. One in every nine Canadian soldiers was hospitalized for treatment of venereal disease.

A little booklet called *Coming Back*, written by Fred J. Smith for the YMCA, grazed the surface of the dilemma of how to return home—and guard against the spoils of heroism. The booklet offered a semi-frank little talk about sexually transmitted diseases, couched in as delicate terms as possible. He reminded the soldiers of the terrible tasks that lay behind them: "During the war your work has been unnatural and destructive."

Ahead, Smith said, there was both glory and danger.

"Heroes are feted, and loved, and flattered by everyone, and some women besides professional prostitutes throw themselves, with all that they possess, at the feet of the men returning from the wars. There is no doubt about it, you can do anything you want with this kind of woman, and it is just here that self-control is a vital necessity. The big man is he who can keep himself clean and pure and true in the midst of undoubtedly strong temptation. The Hero, coming back, must say an emphatic No to the allurements of the flesh... These girls must be protected from themselves, and you men who have shown so much courage and chivalry in your strenuous and victorious opposition of the German hordes will surely be able to act as protectors of this wonderful Canadian maidenhood. Right here you should think very deeply about your attitude toward women. Every child has a right to be well born," Smith urged.

"The Knights of the Round Table rode forth relieving the oppressed and redressing human wrongs. That is to be your duty during the coming years. What have we been fighting for over there?

Well, we have been fighting for liberty and freedom and justice and righteousness, if we have been fighting for anything at all. It was for this that more than 50,000 of our comrades are today lying under little white crosses in France and Flanders. It was for this that thousands of our comrades are maimed and mutilated for life. We surely, then, want liberty and freedom in Canada. But there can be no real freedom and no true liberty in this broad Dominion if the country is enthralled by venereal disease, and bound down by the fetters of immorality."

Despite the warnings, many post-war family men brought venereal disease back to unsuspecting brides.

Literary Fallout

The Great War had a significant impact on the works of some of the top writers of the twentieth century. For the British author of *The Lord of the Rings*, imagery and fierce quests in his early works were foreshadowed on the Western Front, where J.R.R. Tolkien was in the

British army. The 2019 biopic *Tolkien* (directed by Dome Karukoski and written by David Gleeson and Stephen Beresford), draws parallels between his war experience and his work. American author Ernest Hemingway's 1929 novel, *A Farewell to Arms*, centres around an American lieutenant serving in the ambulance corps of the Italian Army. It was inspired in part by his own time spent in the Great War—he too drove ambulances at the Front and had a failed romance there—but the parallels were not connected enough to make it truly autobiographical. Hemingway and another First World War veteran, F. Scott Fitzgerald, author of *The Great Gatsby*, were among those dubbed the "Lost Generation" by literary luminary Gertrude Stein in their post-war Paris literary circle. The moniker stuck for millions of others.

A Round Door

Exploring the former Western Front can lead to unusual sights.

Consider a small canal bank house with a round door, covered in vines and mossy with age. It sounds like a Hobbit home right out of the mind of *The Lord of the Rings* author J.R.R. Tolkien—something he might even have seen, as a Great War veteran himself, or something you might see at the modern but curiously ancient-seeming Hobbiton in New Zealand.

But it was anything but fantasy when tens of thousands of Belgian families were displaced when their homes on the Western Front's "Devastated Zone" were destroyed by shelling. For them, economic hardship and hunger were by-products of the war, Nick Mol, a guide and researcher who lives in Wevelgem, West Flanders, told me.

For example, Mol said, a former British bunker on the canal in Boezinge, West Flanders, became emergency accommodation for an extended family after the war. Behind the odd rounded door was a haven for people who were refugees in their own land.

"Many cities and towns were completely destroyed. The families who had fled from the violence of war returned after the war and had nothing left. It took years before many of the houses were rebuilt in the west corner. Hence, many sought temporary shelter in bunkers and sheds," said Mol.

Relationships That Began under Intense Circumstances

The Western Front might seem hardly the place to meet a marriage prospect, but mixed in with the gunpowder and the stench of death, there were plenty of pheromones and testosterone: love was in the air. For some, "blighty"—a wound serious enough to warrant a trip home or a job away from the dangers of the Front—could be a blessing in more ways than relief from danger. The military hospitals—or leave in towns away from the Front—brought lonely soldiers far from home into close proximity with women, whose own natural prospects were often taken out of the running by the war. Introductions with lasting consequence were sometimes made at a dance, or at church, or as close as a call for a bedpan. Sometimes in the chaos and pain of a protracted hospital recovery from shrapnel injuries, love bloomed. Romance in time of war had an intensity, often buoyed by flurries of letters back and forth.

According to Library and Archives Canada, an estimated 54,000 relatives and dependents accompanied troops returning to Canada through the Department of Immigration and Colonization following demobilization after the First World War. With some 424,000 fellows in Europe or England and tens of thousands hospitalized with wounds by the end of the war, Canadian soldiers were marrying British and European women at the rate of a thousand per month, says genealogist and *War Brides* author Annette Fulford of Maple Ridge, BC. Thousands came in an immigrations scheme: free third-class passage for the dependents of soldiers, paid for by the Canadian government. By August 1919, there were 35,000 new women immigrants.

Bring Her Home

Norman Sydney Richards immigrated to British Columbia with his widowed mother when he was in his teens. When he heard his motherland calling, he returned in 1917 to sign up with the British Army.

Severely wounded at the Front, he spent more than a year in hospital. It was not wasted time: there he found love in the form of the lovely Pearl Cullimore. He married her and brought her home to Salmon Arm.

Salmon Arm Observer journalist Barb Brouwer interviewed Richards's daughter, Esme Farnham, who said shrapnel lodged in his forehead gave him headaches and seizures. He recovered enough to launch agriculture enterprises. When the Second World War broke out, Richards tried to enlist, but he couldn't get a clean bill of health. He didn't speak much about the war, his daughter said.

"He was an officer and a gentleman, a great dad, quiet, fairly strict; [Norman and Pearl] were very good parents," Farnham told Brouwer.

Turning Luck

One bit of bad luck after another turned out well for Hugh McKenzie Clarke. Conscripted away from what had been essential work—farming—he had to leave the family farm at Storthoaks, Saskatchewan, for basic training in Regina. Clarke was shipped to Camp Bramshott in Southern England, and earmarked for service in France. Fate intervened in the form of a germ: the flu pandemic swept through his regiment in August 1918. Fortunately by the time he recovered enough to fight, the fighting was done. He was transferred to Ripon in North Yorkshire in January 1919. A local girl brought him home for dinner, where he met her sister Grace Gibson, a music teacher. By April, Hugh and Grace were married. The pair travelled home to Canada on the *Melita*. Grace adapted to life on the prairies, learning to garden, can, and cook on the woodstove. She taught piano as well. Their granddaughter Annette Fulford kept the pair's letters, and retold their love story.

Promises Fulfilled

Often a sweetheart waited in the wings back home. A young lady named Alice was wooed and won by Bob Hale with notes like this one found on canadianletters.ca: "Please don't worry, darling. I love you with all my heart and soul and I want to marry you. Remember, it is for the freedom of Canada and you that we are fighting. If I go to the Front and get killed, just remember me sometimes. But I think I will live to see you again . . . xxxxxxxxxxxxx." And he did!

10

KEEPING REMEMBRANCE ALIVE

When He Sees: Hill 145 at Vimy

Marc Bétournay visits the Canadian National Vimy Memorial every year. Formerly Canada's chief digging engineer, the Quebec resident sees Vimy differently: he sees tunnels, diggers, Canadian boys making ready for battle. Interviewed while standing at the heights, with its impressive view of the Douai Plain, he sees Vimy's strategic importance in a war that dragged on for years. He sees weak rock and chalk. Havoc among men. He hears explosives, feels the impact of shells on the earth. He sees determination. The creeping barrage. The footsteps in their shoes.

When Bétournay looks at Hill 145, he sees sacrifice of youth. He sees what Vimy knows.

Vimy knows what it costs, this brilliant plan—the creeping barrage of 100,000 Canadians pouring over Vimy Ridge, infantrymen inching carefully. Grim, inexorable, never halting, in the near wake of artillery onslaught from 850 Canadian cannons. A model of Canuck ingenuity.

Vimy knows what the French and British couldn't do alone, taking trench after trench. This relentless Easter push that scars her earth, Hill 145 and its crest, so fetchingly described as "the Pimple."

The memorial's architect was Walter Seymour Allward. After being awarded the competition, it took him eleven years (and $1.5 million, a princely sum then) to build by 1937. It took fifteen thousand tonnes of concrete with hundreds of tonnes of steel reinforcement, many tonnes of Croatian limestone. As the builders dug, they found live shells and bombs, all requiring safe detonation—just a tiny fraction of what had been sown there over a few bitter days in April 1917. More shells are buried still. Up to 400 sheep are allowed to graze on and trim nearby grass, but humans must keep off the grass.

Twenty figures were carved where they stand, in tiny temporary studios, by expert carvers working from half-size plaster models made by Allward.

The tallest figure, Peace, rises 110 metres to gaze eastward over the Douai Plain. The tall columns represent Canada and France, two long-related countries who came together to fight for peace and freedom in the Allied nations. It took a thirty-ton block of limestone just to create the cloaked and hooded woman—*Canada Bereft*, a young country mourning fallen sons.

Other figures represent all those ideals war is supposed to be about. Peace and Justice, Truth, Knowledge, Gallantry, Sympathy. Sacrifice tossing his torch to comrades to carry on. The imagery isn't veiled. A breaking sword. Cannons, draped in branches of laurel and olive—time for Victory and Peace.

On the outside walls, there are the names of 11,285 Canadians killed in France, with no known resting place. From its imposing summit, within a sixteen-kilometre radius, thirty different war cemeteries cradle the bones of 7,000 dead.

What does it all cost? Vimy knows, for she cannot look away: the lives of the 3,600 men planted on that hill, grief for 3,600 families. Loss and rehabilitation for 5,000 wounded. Vimy knows the costs were greater than the sum of all these casualties.

It is said that growing up is the death of fairy tales; it is also said that this happened for Canada in 1917, at Vimy—where Canada was brilliant, her four divisions of the Canadian Corps, side by side, fighting as one.

On everlasting watch on the steps approaching the great pillars, a mother forever holds a stone newspaper with the day's list of casualties.

The 1960s protest song by Pete Seeger asks: Where have all the flowers gone?

Vimy knows. She can see them from here.

Stained Glass and Cigarettes

One stained-glass window at the Anglican church in Kettlewell in the scenic dales of Yorkshire, England, is dedicated to the memory of Lieutenant Charles Godfrey Haggas Cutcliffe Hyne of the Irish Guards. He was the son of a popular British novelist, said blogger John Broom, author of *Fight the Good Fight: Voices of Faith from the First World War.*

"The left panel depicts a soldier on sentry duty on the battlefield. The centre panel depicts a guardian angel standing over discarded military equipment. The right panel depicts a soldier by a camp fire, smoking a cigarette (possibly the only instance of a cigarette appearing

in a church memorial window). In the background are scenes of battle ruins and barbed wire, and an angel appears to be ministering to all the men," said Broom.

The vicar of the church, J.W. Cockerill, presided over the funeral of the lad it's dedicated to. The vicar had his own cross to bear: his own son, Sergeant John Cockerill of the Royal Canadian Dragoons, died earlier that year on February 20, 1916, at Bailleul.

Names without Graves

In modern-day Ieper, a hush sweeps through the arches of the Menin Gate each and every evening at 8:00 PM, precisely. Engraved here are 54,896 names of Commonwealth soldiers missing in action before August 15, 1917, along with the following words: AD MAJOREM DEI GLORIAM. HERE ARE RECORDED NAMES OF OFFICERS AND MEN WHO FELL IN YPRES SALIENT BUT TO WHOM THE FORTUNE OF WAR DENIED THE KNOWN AND HONOURED BURIAL GIVEN TO THEIR COMRADES IN DEATH.

The mournful trumpet of the Last Post echoes. Heads bow. In rain, snow, or the bitterest cold, or the social isolation of the pandemic era, voices fall silent for the moment to remember war's profanity.

Engraved on a massive curved stone wall at Tyne Cot Cemetery near Ieper, the words of British King George V are engraved and dated May 11, 1922:

IN THE COURSE OF MY PILGRIMAGE I HAVE MANY TIMES ASKED MYSELF WHETHER THERE CAN BE MORE POTENT

ADVOCATES OF PEACE UPON EARTH THROUGH THE YEARS TO
COME THAN THIS MASSED MULTITUDE OF SILENT WITNESSES
TO THE DESOLATION OF WAR.

Tyne Cot is the largest Commonwealth cemetery from any war.
Ever. Beneath stark white gravestones, 11,965 lie buried. The memorial
was designed by Sir Herbert Baker, with sculptures by Joseph Armitage,
and Ferdinand Victor Blundstone, who designed the Newfoundland
Memorial. Carved into the curved walls, there are 34,997 names of
Commonwealth soldiers who went missing between August 1917 and
November 1918.

We don't know where the lost are, but we know where to find their
names.

There's a Ring of Remembrance in France, on the hills of Artois,
with 600,000 names of soldiers who fell. It's now the largest military
cemetery in France, the Notre-Dame-de-Lorette International Memorial at Ablain-Saint-Nazaire, Nord Pas-de-Calais. In this encircling of

names, there is no distinction by nationality. No regard for gender. No barriers of religion. A century on, there's an echo of much-needed universal perspective in Philippe Prost's design. It is just humans remembering, humans remembered, with a cloud of witnesses.

The 42nd Rainbow Division

As a "symbol of French–American friendship, a call for peace among nations," a memorial to the 42nd Rainbow Division was erected at Croix Rouge Farm at Fère-en-Tardenois. There, 162 soldiers from Alabama and their Iowa comrades died on July 26, 1918. A bronze soldier carries the body of his dead comrade, forever the witness of the sacrifice of young Americans. According to the site's website, croixrougefarm.org, the memorial artist James Butler recalls his own army experience, and has "a great admiration and sympathy for the lot of the common soldier and how sometimes the most ordinary man will rise to the heights of great bravery and concern for his fellow soldier. In the 42nd Rainbow Division memorial, my original idea was to portray the powerful bond between men on active service with a soldier carrying his dead comrade. However, after working on the sculpture for some time, the piece began to have a strong spiritual meaning for me. The dead soldier is limp, as if his body had just been lifted from the battlefield. The figure holding the dead man began to have the presence of the Angel of Mercy. He is perfect—there are no battle scars on him and he is untouched by the grim conflict. I am not a religious man, but working on this sculpture I felt a strong spiritual guidance."

Soldier Statues

Alan Livingstone MacLeod has made a calling of documenting Canada's Great War memorials. His trek has taken him from the graves of seven of his relatives near where they fell on the Western Front, to coast to Canadian coast. "In Canada, a war memorial can be an arena, clock, or museum. A hospital, column, or tower. A bridge, hall, or gun. An arch, park, or building. A wall, window, or street. And many other things besides," MacLeod writes.

He and his wife Jan have documented the majority of memorials raised to remember the Canadian fallen. His book, *Remembered in Bronze and Stone: Canada's Great War Memorial Statuary*, focuses on the memorials bearing statues of Canadian soldiers—such as the one in tiny Malpeque, Prince Edward Island. Sixteen names on a bronze shield represent the "brave and noble sons who gave their lives for home, empire, and freedom in the war of 1914–1918." Among the names, there are three farmer McGougans. David and John joined the Sixth Canadian Mounted Rifles, one after the other, on August 6, 1915, in Amherst, Nova Scotia. David died December 26, 1918. John died at Vimy Ridge and is buried nearby at Liévin cemetery. George died August 22, 1917 in the Battle for Hill 70 and has no known grave. Atop

the monument's stone base there is a life-sized bronze soldier holding a rifle in his left hand, hoisting a flag with his right, the work of Hamilton Thomas Carlton Plantagenet MacCarthy. "Funds for the memorial are said to have been raised by ordinary people in Malpeque and nearby communities," MacLeod says.

They Shall Not Grow Old

With his imaginative works like *The Jungle Book* and stirring poems like "If," Nobel laureate Rudyard Kipling had the world at the tip of his pen. All at once a realist, a staunch booster of the British Empire, and something of a sentimentalist, Kipling predicted the First World War, according to Ronan McGreevy in the *Irish Times*. Doleful, Kipling warned that continental slaughter was imminent as Europe reached the tipping point.

Still, when his son John, age seventeen and a student at Wellington College, was turned away as unfit to serve in the British army with eyesight so poor he couldn't read the second line of the eye chart without glasses, the elder Kipling sought out in earnest—and finally secured with much effort—an officer post for him with the Irish Guards.

The Irish Guards were at the Battle of Loos. Starting on September 25, 1915, Loos was a disaster for the British. And for the Kiplings.

Second Lieutenant John Kipling was reported missing at Chalk Pit Wood.

"Most families lacked the means or contacts to go searching for their missing relatives on the battlefields. Most families weren't the Kiplings," McGreevy wrote.

Rudyard and his American wife Carrie called in every chip they could. They combed the Western Front, desperate for news of John. They walked the wards of hospitals. They had fliers dropped across German lines. They sought intervention from the royal families of nearby neutral countries, hoping to learn the Germans were holding him as a prisoner of war.

Finally, heartbroken past hope, they learned from a comrade that John Kipling was shot in the head in the shell hole at Chalk Pit Wood, where he lay vaporized by shellfire.

In 1916, Kipling turned to ink to pour his heart out, penning the heart-wrenching poem "My Boy Jack" about Jack Cornwell, who at sixteen was the youngest recipient of the Victoria Cross, dying at his post in the naval Battle of Jutland:

"Have you news of my boy Jack?"
 Not this tide.
"When d'you think that he'll come back?"
 Not with this wind blowing, and this tide.
"Has anyone else had word of him?"
 Not this tide.
 For what is sunk will hardly swim,
  Not with this wind blowing, and this tide.
"Oh, dear, what comfort can I find?"
 None this tide,
  Nor any tide,
Except he did not shame his kind—
 Not even with that wind blowing, and that tide.
 Then hold your head up all the more,
  This tide,
  And every tide;
Because he was the son you bore,
 And gave to that wind blowing and that tide!

At war's end, the elder Kipling would write the shortest, most searing words in his role with the Imperial War Graves Commission: engraved on the memorials, THEIR NAMES LIVETH FOREVER

MORE, and the fervent phrase seen on too many unidentified graves, KNOWN UNTO GOD.

In the little sun-washed town of Oamaru, New Zealand, up on the main drag, away from the harsh surf that pounds at the stone pier, a forty-foot obelisk of Sicilian marble is notched into the busy main drag. Here sculptor T.J. Clapperton's Great War ANZAC soldier is cast in bronze. The man comforts a child, who, legend has it, represents humanity's ideals. The monument is incised with names of local fellows who didn't return from the war. It's all, a bronze panel says, TO OUR GLORIOUS DEAD, AND THOSE WHO SHARED THEIR SERVICE AND SACRIFICE.

The accompanying bronze plate bears a few immortal words from Rudyard Kipling: FROM LITTLE TOWNS IN A FAR LAND WE CAME, TO SAVE OUR HONOUR AND A WORLD AFLAME. BY LITTLE TOWNS, IN A FAR LAND, WE SLEEP, AND TRUST THOSE THINGS WE WON TO YOU TO KEEP. Kipling felt these words deeply, with the fairest of reasons: their names liveth forever more.

A short, unique, poetic New Zealand film aired at the Auckland War Memorial Museum in 2018 traces the journey Maori and Pacific Island soldiers took to war. Filmed at the Britomart station in Auckland, Vanessa Crofskey joined a panel of young poets in *Pou Kanohi: New Zealand at War*. The project combines heart-rending footage of 1918 hakas of grief with next-generation poets recalling the sacrifices of their ANZAC forefathers and asking piercing questions about colonialism and sacrifice. "The epicentre of wartime in New Zealand is the sound of a train departing... open tunnels birth boys to soldiers... Auckland 1914 and the train tracks that are sweeping the nation are the same veins that pump iron pride through our concrete streets."

The director of the *Lord of the Rings* movies, New Zealand's Peter Jackson, took soundless black-and-white Great War footage, slowed down the hectic antique pace that makes all old silent films look faintly comedic, and put sound and colour in to make a new film altogether—with considerable resources. Professional lip readers helped recreate the script of *They Shall Not Grow Old*, and professional voice actors, with accents to match the uniforms, gave the soldiers voices. The result was an engrossing and very human look at the war and those who served. It has cinematic immediacy—an intimacy never seen before except by those who served—and carries the essences of the ANZACs far and wide on a sepia tide.

Remembering Them

On the former Western Front, the past comes back afresh every day. Live explosives are still occasionally killing people who come across them, a century after they were first interred. Intact shells have to be detonated by trained demolition teams. Up pops an ulna in a field of root vegetables: bones are discovered every month, still. Each time, the police have to come inspect some small fragment to make sure they really date to the Great War era and do not belong to some hapless modern-day crime victim. A specialist checks for clues. Is it a German shoelace? A British button? A fragment of leather from an ANZAC hat? A thread from a Turkish colonial's garb? A rusted-out American side-arm? Or some other artifact that can place the tissue fragment with one side or another, for burial purposes—or perhaps even to weave into some episode of *War Junk WWI* on the History Channel? All over the former Western Front, now mild with homes and flowers and fields

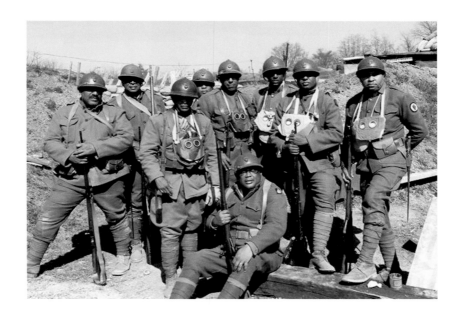

still dimpled with crater lines and creased with trenches, unexploded ordnance that has been secreted works its way to the surface in some farmer's field.

Often as an occupation, but typically for the sheer passion of helping people learn about war, professional guides visit the former battlefields. They document with photos and social media posts, leading descendants to the graves of those who succumbed to war. They illuminate memorials and landmarks, graves dug a century ago. They are modern shepherds, leading descendants, helping people excavate their personal pasts. More than a century later, at the Western Front and the places where people descend from those who fought there, efforts are underway daily to make sure the losses of the Great War are not forgotten.

Tranchée de Chattancourt is an active French First World War frontline trench at Verdun, rebuilt to specs according to original maps, photos, and soldier accounts from 1916. Re-enactors like guide Gerard Brusco are educational anachronisms, living the stories so new generations can understand.

Wearing uniforms styled like those worn by forefathers and armed with research about them, the Ebony Doughboys at the Ypres Cloth Hall in the Grote Markt honoured the sacrifices made by Black American servicemen a century ago, earning them the annual award of the Congressional Black Caucus Veterans Braintrust.

Lisa Oberg curated an exhibit on the fifty-eight students and staff from the University of Washington who died while in service in the First World War. She posted their biographical sketches on Facebook and on *Washington On the Western Front: At Home and Over There*. Among their number, Nicholas Paul Comeford Healy, who was killed when the Curtiss Jenny plane he was piloting in a training flight in La Jolla, California, plunged nose-first at five hundred feet.

British photographer Stephen Kerr of SK Photos uses an ultralight airplane and sometimes a drone to soar above the battlefields of the Western Front and capture their cemeteries' haunting tranquility and echoes of the past. With a bird's-eye view, he uses both stills and video to pass on the perspective of all the rows of crosses and headstones and memorials, settled for a century amid farms and towns of Belgium and France.

The Canadian Letters and Images Project, VIU

At canadianletters.ca, digital remembrance can be accessed, pixel by pixel, from a vast collective brain on demand. Here, classrooms, families, and anyone interested can pore over letters, documents, and memories from soldiers in what Dr. Stephen Davies calls a "small-scale project." His students in the history department at Vancouver Island University scan letters, photos, paybooks, telegrams, journals, and postcards from the First World War. Together, they encapsulate the digital equivalent of shovels and headlamps to mine history, taking discovery and learning beyond books and classrooms.

Davies and his students have put more than 25,000 letters from soldiers online for the public. "It has taken off as a national project," said Davies. "I think the letters are the most powerful means of understanding what the war experience encompassed."

What's online is about half of what has been digitized so far—but the project doesn't receive any government funding, and any donations are used to pay students part-time wages to scan, transcribe, and upload. Davies stresses that no items are retained. The project pays to have them picked up and then returned as soon as they've been respectfully scanned and transcribed.

There are also teacher resources online to encourage classrooms to make the project part of their history learning. Students in Davies's First World War classes can participate in field school programs in Belgium and France, where they can reach out and touch the tombstones of soldiers for whom they've written biographies.

In addition to the First World War, the project covers memorabilia from other eras, including the Second World War and the Korean War. "We're proud of what we've done, and we want to make Canadians aware that it's important to preserve [these items] in some form," Davies said.

Redpatch

Redpatch, a graphic novel illustrated by Christian Kent, is based on a play about an Indigenous Great War soldier, by Raes Calvert and Sean Oliver. It follows a young soldier from the Nuu-chah-nulth Nation of Vancouver Island, and with his peers experiences the horrors of war.

The play *Redpatch* ran at the Citadel theatre in Edmonton in 2018, and in 2019 at the Arts Club in Vancouver.

Redpatch writer and performer Raes Calvert said he was inspired by Henry Louis "Ducky" Norwest, a Métis homesteader and trapper from southern Alberta, who distinguished himself as a First World War sniper with 111 kills to his credit, before he was himself felled by a German sniper.

Calvert was also moved by the story of legendary Ojibway sniper Company Sgt. Maj. Francis Pegahmagabow.

"Indigenous soldiers were used as snipers and trench raiders and scouts. They were very acclaimed for their abilities, based on pre-wartime abilities in surviving outdoors, hunting, tracking," he said.

Calvert hired Robert MacDonald, a war historian from the Seaforth Highlanders regiment, to consult on all things military so the play would have an authentic feel.

"He knew everything—Ypres, Vimy, the Somme, a number of other battles. We wanted to be specific about trench warfare, puttees, knives, trench foot. We wanted to be as historically accurate as possible," Calvert said.

A performer by trade, Calvert played the protagonist in the story, basing him heavily on his own grandfather. Roy Doherty, a Second World War soldier from the Clinton-Lillooet region of British Columbia, was originally from Friendly Cove (Yuquot), northern Vancouver Island. The play incorporates the Mowachaht dialect of that region.

Doherty passed away when Calvert was thirteen.

"I never really got to talk to him about his time in the army. I feel like through doing this play—the research, the development—I do have my grandfather there with me the whole time. I've come to understand him better, many years after his death, which is quite a profound thing," Calvert said.

An English great-grandfather on Calvert's father's side fought in the trenches in the First World War and was wounded by a bayonet, but somehow survived. Calvert wants to learn more about that ancestor's experience; it's what he had in mind when he developed this atmospheric play.

"I tried to recreate what it was like for men in the trenches—the smoke and fog, modernizing something that we, nowadays, can't even project: how terrible and horrible it was for the men and women who had to endure this terrible war," Calvert said.

Percy: A Story of 1918

For those who prefer stories told with lots of pictures, there are a number of graphic novels that use a striking and dramatic comic panel-type format to tell stories of the First World War.

A cache of letters unearthed at a flea market led to a highly illustrated tale of one young man's short war. Conscripted into the Royal Welsh Fusiliers and sent to the Front, Percy Edwards served only three weeks before being killed in action—one of more than 700,000 British soldiers to die in the First World War. Author Peter Doyle combined Edwards's own words from letters with additional narrative material to create *Percy: A Story of 1918* to help young readers imagine what it would be like to find themselves in a foreign country, in a war zone.

The book was shortlisted for the Society for Army Historical Research Fiction Prize.

"Percy's story, whilst being the tale of one young man's short war, had a universal narrative that applied to so many young conscripts of the last year of the war. For both of us the Great War has been a consuming passion for many, many years so it felt almost like a duty to make sure Percy's story was told," said illustrator Tim Godden.

As a project, Godden used the letters of Percy's that were interwoven into Doyle's text to draw out the story. It's not a graphic novel—it's more like illustrated letters with a contextual narrative running in and out.

"For me, the addition of illustrations do a few things. First, they bring Percy to life. There is no known photograph of him, and so this was our opportunity to make him real again. Second, the illustrations are done in a way that means the book will appeal to a younger audience, but also enhance the experience of older readers, too. Finally, it presents the war in colour. Black-and-white photographs have such a wonderful history and storytelling ability of their own, but for me these colour illustrations make the story more immediate, more relatable," he said.

Historian Robert Engen collaborated with the *Hill 70 Memorial Project* to find another way to reach students in Canadian high schools. Historian and illustrator Matthew Barrett Hill then used graphics to tell a visual story from the perspective of Lieutenant Brock Chisholm of the 15th Battalion.

Other graphic novels set in the Great War include Alan Cowsill and Lalit Kumar Sharma's *World War I: 1914–1918*; *Charley's War: 2 June 1916–1 August 1916* by Pat Mills and Joe Colquhoun; *Trenches* by Scott Mills; *It Was the War of the Trenches* by Jacques Tardi; *True Stories of World War I* by Nel Yomtov, Jon Christopher Proctor, and Timothy Solie; *To End All Wars: The Graphic Anthology of the First World War* by Jonathan Clode and John Clark; *The Harlem Hellfighters* by Max Brooks; *Nice Day for a War: Adventures of a Kiwi Soldier in World War I* by Chris Slane and Matt Elliott; *The Great War: July 1, 1916: The First Day of the Battle of the Somme: An Illustrated Panorama,* by Joe Sacco and Adam Hochschild.

Remembered in Tattoos

Steven Van Den Eynde is a walking memorial. It doesn't hurt, he says, as the needle works remembrance in muted tones. This is a real farewell to arms: his flesh engraved with names of men who died, to show his respect for their choice, and for what they had to cope with. For sacrifice given for God, for country, for us, he says. He has visited all of their graves, except for the one in the Dardanelles—it's on his bucket list. The art inked by Mariska Van Lissum of Cirk Tattoo in Aalst, Belgium includes W.A. Curran's epitaph: YEARS ROLL BY, BUT LOVE AND MEMORIES NEVER DIE. The same goes for tattoos.

Kitcheners

From Kitchener, Ontario, to Kitcheners' Wood, store proprietor Steve Douglas has turned a love of Canadian war history into the passion of a lifetime.

Tucked behind the Lewis gun in the window of the British Grenadier Bookshop, the expat Canadian is perfectly poised on the road to the Menin Gate in historic Ieper, Belgium. Once known as Ypres, the quaint village was Ground Zero in the Great War from 1914 to 1918.

Visible from his sidewalk to the right is the impressive gothic cathedral and ancient Cloth Hall—now home to the In Flanders Fields Museum—successfully defended by Canadian troops at great cost in places like nearby Kitcheners' Wood, named after Field Marshal Horatio Herbert Kitchener. And if you look to the left, you will see the Menin Gate. More than a century later there's no more strategic place to be during the post-centenary rush as millions of visitors and students converge on Flanders, Belgium, the restored heart of what was once billed as The War to End All Wars.

"There's loads of Canadian connections in this area," said Douglas, who was born in Britain and raised in Kitchener, Ontario—another location named for Field Marshal Kitchener when its former name, Berlin, fell out of fashion.

Douglas's store is filled with memorabilia and books about the First World War. His tour company brings visitors from Canada and elsewhere to places like Vancouver Corner, Essex Farm, Tyne Cot, and of course, the nearby Menin Gate.

In 1997, Douglas started the Maple Leaf Legacy project, with the goal of capturing photographs of every Canadian war grave and putting them online so even those unable to travel to former battlegrounds could see the graves of the Canadians laid among the Commonwealth dead there.

More than twenty years later, he's still working on it. Eventually, he bought the bookshop and battlefield tour business he worked for, combining his interests in Canadian history, world history, genealogy, computer science, and photography.

"It entirely changed my life," he said.

Many people who come to his door are in Ieper to follow up on family history. Perhaps they've learned they had a relative who served or was killed in the First World War, or they want to try to find a grave or see a name on a memorial, or they want to visit the site of the battle where their relative died.

"You never know who you're going to meet or what kind of artifact is going to come through the door. You meet famous people and unknown people with fascinating stories," Douglas said.

EPILOGUE

Why Shoot a Man You Never Knew?

"The Last Fighting Tommy," Harry Patch was the last surviving combat soldier of the First World War. He died in 2009, aged 111 years, plus one month, one week, and one day. Born and raised in Combe Down, Somerset, England, Patch was injured at Passchendaele on September 22, 1917. No guns were allowed at the funeral of the Last Tommy. Not even a service weapon, not a one. The last surviving soldier of the Western Front had plenty of questions at the end: Harry Patch wanted to know what was logical about a licence to go out and murder, to commit "calculated and condoned slaughter of human beings." Why shoot a man you never knew? Why kill a bloke you never had a quarrel with? Harry Patch wanted to know: If you couldn't even speak his language, why address him with a gun? "All those lives lost for a war finished over a table," he mused.

Lessons from the Western Front

There were terrible things to be learned on the battlefield—things that had to be, but couldn't be. Things that were studiously unlearned later. There are some chestnuts to be gathered a century on from war—that school of the hardest of all possible knocks. Here are life lessons I learned in reading thousands of journals and letters from the Western Front, and from walking on the Western Front:

Take care of your feet. Learn how to mend a rip or a sew a button. Don't be lippy. Mind your step. Keep your head down. Make a will. Write neatly—someone may need to read your words someday. Sometimes it's best to stay put, and sometimes it's best to get out fast; wise is the person who knows the difference.

Keep your kit dry. In lieu of an umbrella or a roof, a rubber sheet or anything will do in a pinch. The hungrier you get, the more willing you are to eat weird combinations of things—in fact, many things will do in a pinch. It could always get worse—you don't want to know how, but sometimes it does. Making lists for the future can help keep you sane when you're in a tough spot. A hot bath is one of life's greatest gifts. Sometimes you really need something to eat. Everyone could use a little R&R now and then. Communications with the home front are a lifeline. Things look different when you're desperate. Enjoy nature, even if it's just a fallen leaf; you will feel a tiny bit better. If you can't do anything about the miles of mud ahead of you, do what you can to make it cozy. Know how to make yourself as comfortable as possible in a tough spot.

Have a happy thought that can comfort you. Don't be too surprised if the lines that were drawn last year are different this year. If you think you're depressed, you may just be in a war zone. There are few things that can't be lost; war is not one of them. Some battles take so much to win, it's a net loss. Prepare yourself for when things get better. There will be things you don't have time or energy to think about now.

Tough times don't last, but tough people do (unless your number's up, then that's it). Sometimes you just have to put one foot in front of the other and keep going. You'll feel better about yourself if you can spare someone else a little dignity. Be there for the person standing beside you in the trench. Be nice if you can; everyone has their own lot to manage. Learn to nap anywhere.

And just because the recruiting poster for Great War Cyclists says RIDE THROUGH BELGIUM IF YOU WANT A QUICK TRIP OVERSEAS—THE MOST COMPLETE TRAINING—THE NATTIEST UNIFORM—SCOUTING, SNIPING, DISPATCH RIDING AND OUT-POST DUTIES—ENLIST TODAY! doesn't make it a good idea.

Just because they didn't call it PTSD doesn't mean that's not what it was.

And like war, life is like milking a cow: if you're lucky, you're still alive—and you get up tomorrow to do it all over again.

ACKNOWLEDGEMENTS

WHEN I WALKED in the footsteps of my grandfathers on the Western Front, I had no idea this book would happen. I am grateful to Peggy Aston for starting me on this journey, and to the grandfathers who helped shape my love of history.

A book with this many moving parts could only happen with the help of a larger community.

My deep gratitude goes to the dream team at Heritage House: Rodger Touchie for his vision; Lara Kordic for kind, steady guidance; Nandini Thaker for brilliant shepherding; editor Renée Layberry for marvellous expertise and patience; Setareh Ashrafologhalai for her talent in giving this book its beautiful design; marketing coordinator Leslie Kenny for staunch support. And to Don Gorman of Rocky Mountain Books for his notice.

My particular appreciate to Stephanie Ann Warner her help and wonderful knowledge, and the brilliant image of Harold Monks Sr. that graces the cover. My gratitude to Lt.-Col. John McCrae for the immortal words of his poem, "In Flanders Fields," which inspired the title, *Heard Amid the Guns*.

More than any other single source, canadianletters.ca, Dr. Stephen Davies and his students at VIU.

My gratitude extends to talented researchers on the modern front-lines of historical research: people like Susan Raby-Dunne, Marc and Patricia Betournay, Bob Shiwak, John Moses, Nick Mol, Yann Castel-not, Annette Fulford, Daphne Vangheluwe, Mary Ann Flores, Richard Houghton, Paul Chapman, Kevin Raistrick, Andy Wright, Peter Ker-varec, Stijn De Naeyer, Johan Declef, Lies dePuydt, Andrew McKay, Jurgen Verhulst, Stephen Kerr, Lucy London, Steven Van Den Eynde, Steve Douglas, Raoul Saesen, Geerhard Joos, Sanchari Pal, Michael Gates, Kathy Gates, Nick Miller, Lizzie Crarer, Tim Godden, Shan-non Olson, Chris Florance, Heather Beattie, Suzanne Hervieux, Stacie Petersen, Mike Vietti, Alison Metcalfe, Heather Colautti, Andrew Webb, Lee Ingelbrecht, Tatiana Bogaert, Hanne Deprince, Johnny Sir-lande, Johan Ryheul, Debbie Cameron, Erin Wilson, Shannyn Johnson, Vincent Lafond, Tish MacDonald, Benny and the Becks, Heather Anne Johnson, Lauren Buttle, Kelly-Ann Turkington, Jim Kempling, Kim Geraldi, Brian Vowel, Raes Calvert, George Hookimaw, David Mitsui, Alan Livingstone MacLeod, the Western Front Association—Pacific Coast Branch.

My writing community made me a better writer on this book: Grace Vermeer, Cynthia Sharp, Derek Hanebury, Patty Sralla, Susan Mistal Baker, Caroline Leavitt. The Alberni Valley Words on Fire team who listened as I brought bits of the Western Front month after month: Stephen Novik, Charlene Patterson, Karl Korven, Micah Gardener. At the Federation of BC Writers, Doni Eve, Bryan Mortensen, Shei-lagh Simpson, Andrea Guldin, Francesca Gesualdi, Ursula Vaira, Bill Arnott and the board. Thanks to The Writers Union of Canada, and PEAVI (Professional Editors Association of Vancouver Island). From my community at SFU's The Writers Studio, always the Fictionistas: Coranne Creswell, Emily Olson, Jennifer Fayloga-Santucci, Liz Laidlaw, Sandi Ilsley, June Hutton.

I owe much to the archives and archivists at Canadian War Museum, Canadian Museum of History, Imperial War Museum, HMCS Alberni Museum, VisitFlanders, Canadian National Vimy Memorial, In Flanders Fields Museum, MMP17 Passchendaele Museum, Talbot House, Red Star Line Museum, Auckland War Memorial Museum, Halifax Citadel, Museum of Vignacourt, Kerry Stokes Foundation, Vancouver Island Military Museum, Tofino Museum, Clayoquot Heritage Museum, Museum Windsor, Ellis County Museum, Yukon Archives, EdithCavell.org, Texas Historical Commission, Archives of Manitoba, Saanich Archives, National WWI Museum and Memorial, Museum of the Great War, Royal British Columbia Museum, National Library of Scotland, Taylor Family Digital Library, Library and Archives Canada, Glenbow Project Libraries and Cultural Resources, University of Calgary, National Airforce Museum of Canada, Nikkei National Museum and Cultural Centre.

For technical assistance: Lisa Kaminski at Sitezeal, Martin Gavin at Adroit Editing, Sally Keefe Cohen.

Love to family advisors and cheerleaders on this project: my siblings Charlie and El, Barb and Rod, Jeri and Fran, Laurel and Bill. In particular, Dr. Lindsey Carmichael, Brad Larson, Ryan Larson, Patrick Larson, and always, my first editor, Gerry Carmichael, for his unflagging support and great judgment.

BIBLIOGRAPHY

"Abraham Slowe: British Jews in The First World War—We Were There Too." British Jews in the First World War: We Were There Too. https://www.jewsfww.uk/abraham-slowe-1310.php.

Atwood, Kathryn J. *Women Heroes of World War I: 16 Remarkable Resisters, Soldiers, Spies, and Medics*. Chicago: Chicago Review Press, Inc., 2016.

Bashow, David L., ed. *Canadian Military Journal*, vol. 8, no. 1 (Spring 2007): http://www.journal.forces.gc.ca/vo8/no1/index-eng.asp.

Bird, Will R. *And We Go On: A Memoir of the Great War*. Montreal: McGill-Queens University Press, 2017.

Bracewell, Maurice Wilfred. "Memoir, Maurice Wilfred Bracewell." Canadian Letters. https://www.canadianletters.ca/collections/all/collection/20729.

Broom, John. "Kettlewell." Fight the Good Fight, March 18, 2016. https://faithinwartime.wordpress.com/tag/kettlewell/.

Brouwer, Barb. "Salmon Arm's Hillcrest Subdivision Named for First World War Veteran." *Salmon Arm Observer*, November 10, 2018. https://www.saobserver.net/community/salmon-arms-hillcrest-subdivision-named-for-first-world-war-veteran/.

Castelnot, Yann. "Native American Veterans and Aboriginal Canadian Veterans." Native American Veterans. Accessed August 7, 2020. http://nativeveterans-en.e-monsite.com/?fbclid=IwAR0T0maNz07MP8zPbHcA6rvQox_um_jnyNbSZM0OjQkG-4buH1x-IjTW0zmE.

Cook, Tim, and J.L. Granatstein. *Victory 1918: The Last 100 Days*. Ottawa, ON: Canadian War Museum, 2018.

Coulthard-Clarke, Chris. "Sandy (Major General Sir William Bridges' Horse): The Australian War Memorial." Australian War Memorial. Accessed August 7, 2020. https://www.awm.gov.au/articles/encyclopedia/horses/sandy.

Davies, Dr. Stephen, ed., The Canadian Letters and Images Project, Vancouver Island University, last modified 2020. canadianletters.ca.

"Detail Victim: Wang Hui Lan." Lijssenthoek Military Cemetery. Accessed August 7, 2020. http://www.lijssenthoek.be/de/address/2720/-295792480020848-wang-huilan-295792480034349-wang-hui-lan.html.

Erickson, Mark St. John. "An Epic Stream of American War Horses and Mules Flowed from World War I Newport News." *Daily Press*, August 14, 2019. https://www.dailypress.com/history/dp-world-war-i-war-horses-and-mules-flowed-through-newport-news-20141126-post.html.

Faryon, Cynthia J. *Mysteries, Legends and Myths of the First World War: Canadian Soldiers in the Trenches and in the Air*. Toronto: James Lorimer & Company Ltd., 2009

Ferrell, Lloyd G. *Ancestors and Descendants of Reuben Showalter*. Bellingham: self-published, 1980.

First World War Commemorations Overseas. Newfoundland & Labrador in the First World War. Newfoundland and Labrador Heritage. Accessed August 7, 2020. https://www.heritage.nf.ca/first-world-war/articles/commemorations-overseas.php.

Forsythe, Mark, and Greg Dickson. *From the West Coast to the Western Front: British Columbians and the Great War*. Madeira Park, BC: Harbour Publishing, 2014.

Fulford, Annette. *War Brides*. Toronto: Dundurn, 2009.

Gates, Michael. "From the Klondike to Berlin: The Yukon in the First World War." *Northern Review*, May 2016. https://thenorthernreview.ca/index.php/nr/article/view/627.

Groom, Winston. *A Storm in Flanders: Triumph and Tragedy on the Western Front*. London: Cassell, 2002.

Hammerton, Sir John. *The Great War… I Was There! Undying Memories of 1914–1918*. London: The Amalgamated Press Ltd., 1939.

Handy, Gemma. "The Caribbean Honours Its Overlooked WWI Soldiers." BBC News, November 7, 2018. https://www.bbc.com/news/world-latin-america-46110120.

Kalvapalle, Rahul. "The Forgotten Muslim Soldiers Who Fought in First World War Trenches for the Allies." Global News, November 12, 2018. https://globalnews.ca/news/4651054/muslim-soldiers-first-world-war/.

Keegan, John. *The First World War*. New York: Vintage Books, 1998.

Kipling, Joseph Rudyard. *Twenty Poems by Rudyard Kipling*. London: Methuen & Co., 1918.

Ladies Home Journal, September 1918, Page 1.

Legion Magazine. *True Canadian War Stories*. Toronto: Prospero Books, 1986.

London, Lucy. *Poets, Writers & Artists on the Somme 1916: A Centenary Collection*. New Brighton, UK: Posh Up North Publishing, 2016.

———. *Women Casualties of the Great War in Military Cemeteries, Vol. 1: Belgium & France*. New Brighton, UK: Posh Up North Publishing, 2016.

MacLeod, Alan Livingstone. *From Rinks to Regiments: Hockey Hall-of-Famers and the Great War*. Victoria, BC: Heritage House Publishing Co. Ltd., 2018.

———. *Remembered in Bronze and Stone: Canada's Great War Memorial Statuary*. Victoria, BC: Heritage House Publishing Co. Ltd., 2016

Marshall, Debbie. *Firing Lines: Three Canadian Women Write the First World War*. Toronto: Dundurn, 2017.

Marshall, Debbie. *Give Your Other Vote to the Sister: A Woman's Journey into the Great War*. Calgary: University of Calgary Press, 2007.

Mattick, Lindsay & Josh Greenhut. *Winnie's Great War*. New York: Harper Collins, 2018.

McClary, Donald R. "The Angel of the Trenches." *Catholic Stand*, July 6, 2016. https://catholicstand.com/the-angel-of-the-trenches/.

McCrae, John. "In Flanders Fields." Poetry Foundation, 2020. https://www.poetry foundation.org/poems/47380/in-flanders-fields.

McGreevy, Ronan. "Rudyard Kipling's First World War Tragedy." *The Irish Times*, May 5, 2015. https://www.irishtimes.com/culture/heritage/rudyard-kipling-s-first-world-war-tragedy-1.2190731.

Morpurgo, Michael. *War Horse*. London: Kaye & Ward, 1982.

Nedelman, Michael. "PTSD Risk May Be Inherited through DNA." CNN, April 25, 2017. https://www.cnn.com/2017/04/25/health/ptsd-trauma-genetics-study/index.html.

Pal, Sanchari. "This Forgotten Pilot Was Just 19 When He Became India's First and Only Flying Ace." The Better India, September 14, 2017. https://www.thebetterindia.com/115388/indra-lal-roy-indian-flying-ace-world-war-2/.

Paul, Robert Rollo. "Memoir, Robert Rollo Paul." The Canadian Letters and Images Project. Vancouver Island University. Accessed August 7, 2020. https://www.canadianletters.ca/collections/all/collection/20897/doc/225.

Peat, Harold. *Private Peat*, Bobbs Merrill, 1917.

Peat, Louisa Watson. *Mrs. Private Peat*, Indianapolis, IN: Bobbs-Merrill, 1918.

Raby-Dunne, Susan. *Bonfire the Chestnut Gentleman*. Turner Valley, AB: MMWG (Monday Morning Writers Group), 2012.

———. *John McCrae: Beyond Flanders Fields*. Victoria, BC: Heritage House Publishing Co. Ltd., 2018.

———. *Morrison: The Long-Lost Memoir of Canada's Artillery Commander in the Great War*. Victoria, BC: Heritage House Publishing Co. Ltd., 2017.

Rodricks, Dan. "The Sad, Senseless End of Henry Gunther." *The Baltimore Sun*, October 26, 2018. https://www.baltimoresun.com/news/bs-xpm-2008-11-11-0811100097-story.html.

Savage, Charles Henry. "Memoir, Charles Henry Savage." The Canadian Letters and Images Project. Vancouver Island University. Accessed August 7, 2020. https://www.canadianletters.ca/content/document-8359.

Service, Robert. *Rhymes of a Red Cross Man*. London: T. Fisher Unwin, 1923.

"Women, The Wounded And The War: How WWI Paved The Way For Suffrage." Forces Network, February 6, 2018. https://www.forces.net/news/women-wounded-and-war-how-wwi-paved-way-suffrage.

Sudbury, John P. "Memoir, John P. Sudbury." The Canadian Letters and Images Project. Vancouver Island University, 2018. https://www.canadianletters.ca/content/document-2545?position=1.

Summerby, Janice. *Native Soldiers, Foreign Battlefields*, Veterans Affairs Canada, 1998.

Summerby, Janice, and Veterans Affairs Canada. "Thousands Volunteer." February

14, 2019. https://www.veterans.gc.ca/eng/remembrance/those-who-served/indigenous-veterans/native-soldiers/first_response.

Tamblyn, Lt.-Col. David Sobey. *Horse in War and Famous Canadian War Horses.* Kingston, ON: The Jackson Press, 1932.

"The MacLeod [Alberta] Spectator." *The MacLeod Spectator*, December 2, 1915, Page 1.

The Royal Anglian and Royal Lincolnshire Regimental Association. "The Royal Anglian & Royal Lincolnshire." The Lincoln Branch of The Royal Lincolnshire and Royal Anglian Regimental Association. http://www.thelincolnshireregiment.org/beechey.shtml.

Thorn, Major J.C., *Three Years a Prisoner in Germany.* Vancouver: Cowan & Brookhouse Ltd., 1919.

Tuchman, Barbara. *The Guns of August.* New York: Random House, 1962.

———. *The Zimmerman Telegram.* New York: Random House, 1958.

University of British Columbia Yearbook. Vancouver: UBC Press, 1917.

Veterans Affairs Canada. "Indigenous Veterans." Veterans Affairs Canada, July 15, 2020. https://www.veterans.gc.ca/eng/remembrance/history/historical-sheets/aboriginal-veterans.

Williams, Chad. "What Came After World War I for African-American Veterans." *Time*, November 12, 2018. https://time.com/5450336/african-american-veterans-wwi/.

Interviews

Betournay, Marc. Interview with Jacqueline Carmichael, 2018.

Calvert, Raes. Interview with Jacqueline Carmichael, January 29, 2020.

Davies, Dr. Stephen. Interview with Jacqueline Carmichael, 2018.

Douglas, Steve. Interview with Jacqueline Carmichael, 2018.

Flores, Mary Anne. Interview with Jacqueline Carmichael, August 2018.

Fulford, Annette. Interview with Jacqueline Carmichael, 2018.

Godden, Tim. Interview with Jacqueline Carmichael, January 7, 2020.

Hookimaw, George, interviewed by Jacqueline Carmichael, January 2020.

Johnston, Heather Anne. Interview with Jacqueline Carmichael, May 2020.

Joos, Geerhard. Interview with Jacqueline Carmichael, 2018.

Kerr, Stephen. Interview with Jacqueline Carmichael, 2018.

London, Lucy. Interview with Jacqueline Carmichael, 2018.

Mol, Nick. Interview with Jacqueline Carmichael, 2018.

Moses, John, interviewed by Jacqueline Carmichael, January 2020.

Oberg, Lisa. Interviewed by Jacqueline Carmichael, October 2018.

Raby-Dunne, Susan. Interviewed by Jacqueline Carmichael, January 2020.

Reddan, Kimberley. Interviewed by Jacqueline Carmichael, August 2018.

Saesen, Raoul. Interview with Jacqueline Carmichael, 2018.

Shiwak, Bob, Interviewed by Jacqueline Carmichael, January 2020.

Van Den Eynde, Steven. Interview with Jacqueline Carmichael, 2018.

Warner, Stephanie Ann. Interview with Jacqueline Carmichael, May 2020.

INDEX